Mary Drummond
9/92

WOMEN AND AG
CELEBRATING OUR!
Ruth Raymond Tho

D0430288

SOME ADVANCE REVIEWS

"Out of the experience of her own aging and that of friends, Ruth Thone has created a very solid, courageous and illuminating exposition, leading us relentlessly into the vortex of an issue which swirls around each woman whether she wishes it to or not. She gently nudges women toward taking their aging process in their own hands, urging them to honor who they are and relish the newness and freedom which the last third of their lives can provide, including humor, joy, forgiveness, and celebration."

Katherine P. Riddle, PhD
Professor Emerita
University of Nebraska

"Ruth Thone, with characteristic courage and honesty, writes from her own rich life experiences, from those of participants in her workshops on aging and values clarification, and her extensive literary background. Her interesting and well-written book is a radical invitation to women to take charge of the last third of our lives, with support and affirmation from one another, and thus create a society in which older women can become our authentic selves."

Sr. Adrian M. Hofstetter, PhD
Coordinator, Home Sharing Opportunities, Ulster County
Formerly Chaplain, Creighton University

NOTES FOR PROFESSIONAL LIBRARIANS AND LIBRARY USERS

This is an original book title published by Harrington Park Press, an imprint of The Haworth Press, Inc. Unless otherwise noted in specific chapters with attribution, materials in this book have not been previously published elsewhere in any format or language.

CONSERVATION AND PRESERVATION NOTES

The paper used in this publication meets the minimum requirements of American National Standard for Information Sciences — Permanence of Paper for Printed Material, ANSI Z39.48-1984.

Women and Aging
Celebrating Ourselves

HAWORTH Women's Studies
Ellen Cole, PhD and Esther Rothblum, PhD
Senior Co-Editors

New, Recent, and Forthcoming Titles:

When Husbands Come Out of the Closet by Jean Schaar Gochros

Prisoners of Ritual: An Odyssey into Female Circumcision in Africa by Hanny Lightfoot-Klein

Foundations for a Feminist Restructuring of the Academic Disciplines edited by Michele Paludi and Gertrude A. Steuernagel

Hippocrates' Handmaidens: Women Married to Physicians by Esther Nitzberg

Waiting: A Diary of Loss and Hope in Pregnancy by Ellen Judith Reich

God's Country: A Case Against Theocracy by Sandy Rapp

Women and Aging: Celebrating Ourselves by Ruth Raymond Thone

A Woman's Odyssey into Africa: Tracks Across a Life by Hanny Lightfoot-Klein

Women's Conflicts About Eating and Sexuality: The Relationship Between Food and Sex by Rosalyn M. Meadow and Lillie Weiss

Anorexia Nervosa and Recovery: A Hunger for Meaning by Karen Way

Women and Aging
Celebrating Ourselves

Ruth Raymond Thone

Harrington Park Press
An Imprint of The Haworth Press, Inc.
New York • London • Norwood (Australia)

ISBN 1-56023-005-3

Published by

Harrington Park Press, an imprint of The Haworth Press, Inc., 10 Alice Street, Binghamton, NY 13904-1580

© 1992 by The Haworth Press, Inc. All rights reserved. No part of this work may be reproduced or utilized in any form or by any means, electronic or mechanical, including photocopying, microfilm and recording, or by any information storage and retrieval system, without permission in writing from the publisher. Printed in the United States of America.

Library of Congress Cataloging-in-Publication Data

Thone, Ruth Raymond.
    Women and aging : celebrating ourselves / Ruth Raymond Thone.
      p. cm.
    Includes bibliographical references and index.
    ISBN 1-56023-005-3 (pbk. : acid free paper)
    1. Aged women – United States – Psychology. 2. Aging – Social aspects – United States.
3. Ageism – United States. I. Title.
[HQ1064.U5T46 1992b]
305.4 – dc20
                                            91-19330
                                             CIP

To that longtime friend who, as he laughingly and unwittingly suggested that he is growing old disgracefully, spoke the heart of my book.

ABOUT THE AUTHOR

Ruth Raymond Thone is a writer, teacher, community activist, and speaker. She has been active in progressive politics for many years. Currently, she studies Spanish, records her dreams, travels to see her three grown daughters, and lives in Lincoln, Nebraska, with her husband Charles. She works at a House of Hospitality and a Soup Kitchen, is active in Common Cause, drug and alcohol abuse recovery, anti-war and peace groups, feminist causes, and leads groups in Values Clarification and Realization, Appearance and Aging Issues for Women, and Writing. She is a member of and active in several social justice organizations.

CONTENTS

Preface   ix

I. UNMASKING OUR OWN TRUTH AS AGING
   WOMEN

    Chapter 1. "Just Fine, Thank You."   3

    Chapter 2. Beware the Positivists!   7

    Chapter 3. Aging Gracefully   13

    Chapter 4. LOOKS   19

    Chapter 5. Call It by Its Name   25

    Chapter 6. Just Try Harder   29

    Chapter 7. Women's Work   33

II. ANGER, HURT, GRIEF, AND CHANGE: FACING
   OURSELVES

    Chapter 8. Who Am I Going To Be When I Grow Up?   41

    Chapter 9. Who Am I?   47

    Chapter 10. Internalized Ageism   53

    Chapter 11. The Grief of Aging   57

    Chapter 12. Becoming Old   61

    Chapter 13. Reflections on a Funeral   65

    Chapter 14. Litany of a Death   69

Chapter 15. Where Does the Time Go?   81

Chapter 16. A January Tale   85

Chapter 17. Regret, Oh Damned Regret   89

III. HONORING AND GATHERING OUR STRENGTH

Chapter 18. Interdependence: Support Groups   95

Chapter 19. Heroines: Role Models   99

Chapter 20. Being Response/able   103

Chapter 21. Overall Wellness   107

Chapter 22. To Risk or Not To Risk   111

Chapter 23. Tools   117

Chapter 24. Our Forgiveness Journey   121

Chapter 25. Before the Casket Closes   125

Chapter 26. Celebration   131

Epilogue   137

Bibliography   139

Reading List   145

Index   149

Preface

Old women are mostly invisible in our country. If not ignored, they are pitied, derided, discounted, or feared, unless they are in the socially-acceptable roles of caretaking, that of grandparent or dutiful daughter, or have managed to be considered wise, often because they are rich and/or famous.

We are afraid of aging, because of its powerlessness, its increasing body disabilities and malfunctions, its smells, its oddness, its inability to race around, be important, and to take care of itself. Such characteristics are present at any age, but especially scorned in the old. Our society fears old women because they represent death and disdains them because they are no longer useful, sexually or as caretakers.

In past ages, old women were looked on as wise, powerful, guardians of life's entrances and exits, healers, seers, and truth-speakers. Women's power was taken from them by church fathers, businessmen, university intellectuals, medical doctors, male undertakers, by a gradual, specific, purposeful decision and act of taking unto the male gender those occupations and activities done for ages by women. Inquisitions and witch-burnings are two of the most visible examples of a centuries-long process of taking from women, especially old women, their work, their power, any authority in life.

"There's an aging mystique in this country that is just as serious, and even more pernicious, than the feminine mystique," says Betty Friedan. "It denies reality, and distorts it. It becomes a self-fulfilling prophecy that keeps us from confronting the real possibilities and problems of the new third of life that is now open to people" (Svitil 1990, p. 74).

Pitiful and powerless as we are, is it not strange that old women are still hated and feared?

Who wants to read further?

We do, those of us who are sick and tired of being patronized, who want to add our collective weight and energy to redressing the balance, who refuse to accept our culture's lie that old is ugly. We want to reclaim for ourselves that last third of our lives, supported and affirmed by one another and the society we live in.

This is not a gerontological study, bolstered by statistics and footnotes, although many of the experiences related here can be found in the writings listed at the end of the book.

I tell the story of how some aging and old women are carving out a way of life, hacking their way through the nearly impenetrable undergrowth of our culture's revulsion against us, finding in each other's stories and shared experiences the courage to reclaim our equality not only with aging men, but with the youth so worshipped in this country. At first I wrote of "we" and "us." Reminded that I do not speak for all others, I have tried to avoid the editorial, inclusive and/or bombastic "we," which often results in awkward phrasing.

In the midst of my own aging process, a friend and I designed an hour's presentation to help participants get in touch with their aging concerns and find ways to face them. Later I expanded the work into an eight-week class, laced with the concepts and strategies I have studied and taught in Values Clarification/Realization work for a long time. Since then, I have led groups in churches, renewal centers, religious coalitions, and a community college so women can become conscious of their own aging process and that of the culture in which they live.

I am a white, middle-class woman, living and working in Lincoln, Nebraska, where people of color are less than three percent of the population. Even so, I can remember in the groups, a Native American woman, a woman of Spanish heritage, a differently-abled woman, a friend who is lesbian, and a young woman dentist who is Jewish. That is not much diversity; sometimes ethnocentrism is a reality. However, becoming aware of the oppression of old women has made me more aware of other oppressions, those of poor, lesbian, differently-abled women, and women of color. The work of social justice and peace has taken up much of my energy for the past 10 years, a special consciousness of my own aging years.

Nebraska authors Willa Cather, Mari Sandoz, and another favorite woman writer, Elizabeth O'Connor, all tell us to write of what we know, of our own experience. I have done that, trying not to be insensitive to the concerns of women of different births, backgrounds, lifestyles, and circumstances.

Every page of this book was written intuitively, from my life, my experiences, my feelings. Thus the pattern may not be clear, nor each chapter perfectly organized nor of the same emotional intensity or clarity. It is simply the reflection of one woman's aging, made stronger and braver by reflections and life experiences of other women, both read and heard. The idea is to read and think, remembering and knowing your own story, seeing your own journey as worthwhile, making those choices appropriate to your own situation.

Many women have taken this journey before me, perhaps with less anger and concern about what one's culture says is appropriate. My focus is on the reasons we need and the ways we practice daily affirmative action in the face of subtle, deep, pervasive, unspoken distaste and derision for old people in general and old women in particular in the United States. If you think I exaggerate, please watch television carefully for several days and read some popular magazines.

This is a suggested pathway—books to read, things to do, matters to clear up, our lives to reflect upon and change—for living to old age and affirming ourselves every step of the way.

I understand that not all women have the choices available to me and the women I have worked with. Nor does celebration seem appropriate to women sick, poor, alone, mentally or emotionally disturbed, disabled, or helpless. These conditions can describe people at any age, yet are also often part of the life situation of old women. I'm convinced that as we work to change society's attitudes towards old women, we enlarge the possibilities and improve conditions for all women. It sounds trite to say that we must both respect the diversity of women and live in solidarity with each other, yet I think that is the truth of our lives—all women, whether they are of color, lesbian, poor, differently-abled, or white, middle-class, honoring our differences and hearing and respecting each other's stories and experiences.

The chapters in this living will are based on the areas of our lives

I have found we need to concentrate on, based on the life experiences of many women gathered in groups to reflect and work on their own aging. They are also based on the written work I have found that speaks directly to old women and their status today. Some of the best writing, I think, is by lesbian women, who, surely because of the oppression they know so well, see more directly and face more honestly the ageism in our culture and the very real aging concerns of all women.

I try to avoid giving advice — saying there is one way to feel or think or act — or age! We all have our deep-seated reasons for what we do. I especially try to avoid that shoal of advice that tells us to deny that there is anything wrong in our lives, to deny our feelings of sadness or grief or inadequacy, to smile, because our culture demands cheerfulness, extroversion, activity, or positive thinking.

The work comes directly from my need to record my own aging and the journey of hundreds of sisters through their aging years. It is offered to women wondering how to feel good about themselves, surrounded by all types of media that show images of thin, happy, well-coiffed and dressed, financially-secure, heterosexual-coupled, active, self-confident women.

Where are the real old women? They are everywhere if we would only look and care. We learn to care about ourselves as we age, not to wait until we are old-old, but to begin the journey now. This record is hardly complete; it is a starting place, a reminder to women of reflections and actions that will lead to affirming and celebrating ourselves now and whenever it is we think we are old.

Adrienne Rich (1985, p. 65.) says "The most important thing one woman can do for another is to illuminate and expand her sense of actual possibilities. . . ." This work is offered in that spirit.

I. UNMASKING OUR OWN TRUTH AS AGING WOMEN

Chapter 1

"Just Fine, Thank You."

Some women have spent their lives working hard, at a paid job, keeping up the home front, or both; caring for children, tending to life's details, loose ends, and unfinished business, managing to look good at the same time. Adrienne Rich (1977, p. xvi) calls it "this activity of world protection, world preservation, world repair. . . ." Looking good means that a woman should be clean, tidy, reasonably fashionable, pleasant, optimistic, and kempt. Certainly this generalization has its flaws; it is my observation and reflection, however, that across occupations, races, lifestyles and classes, women in the United States are the peacemakers, the face-savers, the solution-finders, all of which is reflected in our female demeanor.

Unfortunately, this is all too easily translated into a false, mechanistic, culturally-affirmed, life-denying attempt to keep all problems under the surface, under control, and stuffed inside tightly-regulated exteriors. Little girls and grown women are told to smile. We reply "Just fine, thank you," or at least pleasantly, to the occasionally sincere, more often routine, "How are you?" Of course, "How are you?" is often a greeting, not a question, and does not require a litany of one's life and complaints in return.

Visiting my mother late one winter, I proudly showed her a picture of myself in my town's newspaper, a picture taken at a legislative hearing. She took one quick look at this photograph of her youngest daughter, age 57, and retorted: "You look like you're a thousand years old." (Much later I realized she felt very old that day.) My mother did not know that my solemn face was in response to a hearing on the death penalty. Yet even as I expressed disagreement to her strong reaction, she countered, "But you look so serious, dear." Then I remembered — oh, how I remembered — that one is supposed to smile in public — public meaning any time another is around — and to look pleasant at all costs.

Do we learn that iron rule so as to attract the attention and approval of men? Is much of women's behavior drilled into them by hierarchical systems? Is appearing pleasant a social convention used in order not to burden each other with our problems? Does our society need a collective positivism in order not to break down under the weight of individual and collective anxieties and depressions? Do we make our companions think we are "just fine" so that they will trust us in friendship and business? Or is it just one of the ways we manage social interactions in order to glide by one another with the least amount of friction?

For girl-children, and for adult women, the idea is to be pleasant, especially to another. Boys and men have their own set of disabling messages to struggle with. This is not to discount their journey but to understand that for women, the cultural messages say: conform, be pleasant, adorn, do not show strong feelings or exhibit thoughts of substance. This is not as true as it used to be, but it is still the stereotype against which many women struggle.

One spin-off from the "I'm just fine, thank you" school is the gigantic "cosmetic" industry in this country, which encourages women to diet (itself an 11-billion dollar industry), to dye their hair, to have surgery on thighs, stomachs, breasts, and faces, to make up faces in order to be beautiful and desirable, to be ashamed of natural body odor, to wear high heels to make legs "look attractive," i.e., thin, and to have the buttocks wiggle, and to dress in a manner that reflects outside approval, not inner comfort.

Another spin-off is the ascendance of the positive thinkers; the New Age "everything is just fine if you think it is," plus the Christian emphasis on the sun, the western emphasis on extroversion, on coping and producing, and relegating the dark, quiet, mournful, angry, wild side of ourselves to a realm of shame. It is as if the restful, healing nighttime of the moon and our depressions and sorrows can only be shown in private, by women revealing this side of their real selves in moments of solitary candor.

I understand the power and wisdom of affirmations and that we project onto the world our inner realities, created from the inside out and getting back the evidence of what we believe. Yet we must find the courage to be ourselves, expecially in the face of these spiritual truths and to offer that acceptance to one another. To say that everything is operating "just as it should," or that "everything is going to turn out all right," reflects, at a profound level, the actual fact of things. However, women need to include in that "all rightness" their own darkness, and claim to what has been driven underground—the restoring power of darkness, the power of seeds growing in dark soil away from the sunlight, babies growing in the dark of mothers' wombs, the powerful regenerative force of the moon.

I caught myself today projecting my fear of my own inner demons on another. My husband came home tired, uncommunicative, silent, heavy, isolated from me by low energy and lethargy. I became restless and irritated, as if he had no right to be that way around me. Frightened and dismayed by my denial behavior in order to avoid my own depression, I fought against the evidence of such feelings in him. Thus I understand my strong reaction against people who insist that "Just fine, thank you" is the best and most appropriate response to life.

The next three chapters focus on the effects of the "just fine" rule: the first a working out of my feelings when I noticed a group of "feel no regret" women taking over a roomful of women reflecting on regret. The second is a telling experience about "aging gracefully," and the third a concentration on the "cosmetics" of aging, hardly cosmetic in one sense of that word. Dignified speech to the contrary, I call this significant subject "LOOKS." Joining the long list of "isms" to which we are being made conscious, it is called "Looks-ism."

Being clear inside ourselves and choosing whether and how to communicate that clarity to others, resisting the blame-the-victim trap of some forms of thought with its fierce insistence on peace and positivism, aging any way we want to and can, and becoming free of the insidious power of judgement of our appearances—these are the issues that came alive for me when I awakened in my middle-class middle age.

Chapter 2

Beware the Positivists!

The pretty white-haired woman, full of energy and not at all timid about speaking her mind, clenched her fist in the air as she exhorted her classmates to ignore regret and push on with their lives.

Other women in the class joined her cause, murmuring assent, as they leaned forward in their chairs to get in on the idea of not giving regret power in their lives. Only later did I notice that not everyone joined in the regret-bashing. One articulate extroverted woman said to me at the end of the class, "Oh, I regret everything," naming things she regretted that very day.

I'd fallen into the trap of applauding the women who said they spent no time regretting anything and who told the rest of us we shouldn't either. Positive thinking, with its New Age relatives of "creating your own world" and "feeling only love," can be a trap for me and can make me think that how I feel is somehow wrong.

Growing up in a religion that emphasized the good, and taught that "sin, sickness and death are unreal," has left me with a deep need to recognize the world's and my own darkness. I do not go around in a slough of despair, even though I know depression and see the effects of violence and structural and personal injustice. What I take issue with is the marching philosophy that we create reality by our thinking and that we can love our way through problems of war and starvation, hatred and domination. I believe that if we are resentful and bitter, we will draw experiences to us that reinforce that attitude. Yet I do not agree that justice and peace will come to the world if we all just sit in our corners and get our own thinking straight. Such personalism goes against the fact that billions of us inhabit this planet, creating the need to live in community.

Performer Ronnie Gilbert says it well:

> Looking back, what terrifies me is seeing that there have been years and years where the major thrust in personal growth and politics is taking care of oneself, finding the "inner self." This is all very important, but what about our nature as human beings in the community? We are in this world together, and we are either going to make it together or we're not going to make it. (Mitchell 1990, p. 34)

There are things to be sad about, not only in our own remembered pasts but in the world today. We don't make such things more or less real by our attitudes toward them, nor do we want to live weighed down with wrongs and regrets. Not to face and recognize our own sadness and the pain of others seems to me to exhaust us with denying it, and lets it fester inside ourselves. Keeping such darkness at bay gives it greater power over us than does admitting and confronting it.

We say to one another "think positively," "be done with the past," and—in our class of aging women—"damn regret, full speed ahead."

Those of us not exhorting our companions to look on the bright side are the bad guys these days. During meetings, we are the ones who try to voice what we see going on in the group's collective mind and speak the unspoken when the group begins racing on a course of "niceness." Like those of us in the class who kept quiet, thinking we were wrong or should not speak when the positive thinkers took over, and later expressed how we really felt, contrary to the others' evangelism. When I feel or know the pain of a situation, or feel differently than the person expressing the official story, I need to say so, without labeling myself the group grump or depressive. My heart leapt when I heard psychiatrist, author and feminist Jean Shimoda Bolen (1990) say, at a retreat, "The group always needs the voice of what is not being said. It is always a relief when it is said."

To demonstrate that we seekers are not always cheerful and smiling, I show people in my Values Clarification groups two photographs—one of an aging activist now dead, Abbie Hoffman, and the other of his former partner, Jerry Rubin. Rubin is well-dressed, probably makes a considerable salary, and no longer acts out the radical politics of his youth. Hoffman, as we know, was still at it to the end, leading strikes, sit-ins, and rallies, and was deeply involved in social justice work. In the picture, he looks raggedy in a T-shirt and graying beard.

I could also show my groups the full-page picture of myself that appeared in a Women's Campaign Fund promotional brochure years ago. Strangely enough, I felt no shame or discomfort that my photograph was used to represent the unrealized woman. The eyes in these photographs tell us something, the direct, insouciant look of Rubin contrasted with the the vulnerable, sad look on Hoffman's face, and the pain, bewilderment and despair one might see in my face. Seekers are often sad, my old teacher used to say. Afraid of that kind of wisdom, some exhort the rest of us to put an acceptable covering on our truth, even to accept that our facade determines our fate.

I doubt that we seekers of equal opportunity for the long-denied darkness will organize, demanding that others accept our truth. We are people of the edges, knowing one another in our marginated condition in this land of extroversion and positive thinking, carrying the "gift" of not being devastated by darkness yet knowing the price of carrying it, of being labeled negative.

Our voices sound in the wilderness like that of the migrating cranes we hear in the spring, sounding their strange noises high overhead, full of power to make us attend for a moment, bringing a sense of something not understood, a call to a journey not chosen.

The collective unwillingness to face institutionalized and systemic ageism, to face the fears and shames of aging often takes over with a vengeance. It is important to work through regrets and sorrows. A positive attitude may not be the only antidote to loss of productivity, friends, financial security, health, coping abilities, and apparent attractiveness.

Other attitudes, I've learned, can serve as well. Women can speak their fears, write about regrets, admit depression, ask for and give help, and support one another. We can make changes in our culture's discounting of old women. Power is reclaimed by facing the truth about ourselves and the institutions that affect us, not by accepting new or old myths that tell us to smile, to say "just fine, thank you," or to be happy and not to worry, even, in the face of injustice and sorrow. We become whole women in claiming and knowing both our darkness and our light.

I began an "Antidotes to Positivism" list the other day; things to keep myself from becoming a prig, from pretending to be someone I am not, someone who has her own way of being grateful in the world. Years ago a friend sent me this quote from Ted Rubin's *Love me, Love My Fool* (1976, p. 11):

> I must learn to love the fool in me . . . the one who feels too much, talks too much, takes too many chances, wins sometimes and loses often, lacks self-control, loves and hates, hurts and gets hurt, promises and breaks promises, laughs and cries. It alone protects me against that utterly self-controlled, masterful tyrant whom I also harbor and who would rob me of human aliveness, humility, and dignity but for my fool.

These are some of the ways I stay centered, without resorting to positive thinking:

- Petting the cats
- Being glad to be alive
- Alone time
  Laughing until my body aches and my face is drenched with tears
- Saying my truth
  The shortened version of the Serenity Prayer
- A good book
- A quiet walk in shade in summer or sun in winter
  Smelling linden trees blooming
  Seeing the periwinkle chicory blossoms in hot summer
- Writing a letter
- Picking flowers
- An hour of TV, mostly nature or biography documentaries
  Bawdiness
  Hilarity

Being naked
Spending a day in my bathrobe
• Going to a movie
Leaving the house without doing the dishes
Eating popcorn and not caring about spilling
Taking 10 minutes between things on busy days
• Puttering around my house

Surely there are more. Some days my negative filter needs severe adjusting, and I must find the positive side of things. Except for those times, though, I must find my own way through the smog of positivism. Old women, in particular, must find ways of being ourselves, not allowing constant exhortions to be cheerful to rob us of our deepest, truest selves.

Chapter 3

Aging Gracefully

At a Women and Aging class, Miriam described her Aunt Caroline, who at age 102 lived in a nursing home, was visited by numbers of descendants and was "aging gracefully." One woman interrupted to ask Miriam what she meant by "aging gracefully." Savoring the image of Aunt Caroline, the women began to define that common phrase.

The descriptions given included: to be flexible, loving, a lady, positive, appreciative, accepting, tidy, active, open-minded, optimistic, proud of one's achievements, to have a zest for life, inner beauty, a sense of humor, to still learn and take risks, and not to complain of one's aches and pains or other's faults, and not to worry about old age.

The leader interrupted the naming of attributes to ask: "How many of us exhibit these qualities right now?" The women looked startled. More such questions filled the uneasy silence: "Do we ask of our older sisters things we do not expect of ourselves? What burden do we project on aging people, both around us and inside of ourselves? What perfection do we demand of the old?" The room was quiet as each woman faced the questions and began to recognize some of her own internalized ageism.

The culture's collective denial system is difficult to break through. The majority of religions tell us that death can be transcended; funeral practices protect the living from a dead body looking dead, with cosmetics and chemicals, and from handling the burial rituals. For the most part, hospitals and nursing homes hide what dying looks like. Fear of the process of dying and death, of the ego's end, leads us to ignore the old and still project on them much of our own fear.

I suppose it may be possible to "age gracefully" when one is not poor, or alone, or sick of mind or body, or ignored or despised, *and* has lived a privileged life. "Growing old disgracefully" feels healthier and more fun to me, as it is explored in a lovely essay by Maxine White in the June 1990 *Matrix* (pp. 4, 5), a feminist newspaper in Santa Cruz, CA. White, who directs the Women's Center at Cabrillo College, writes:

> If growing old gracefully means not aiming for one's craziest dreams, then I want no part of it. . . . Anyone who is still curious about the world could never be content to grow old gracefully.
> Perhaps that is the crux of growing old disgracefully: you disentangle yourself from the identity and opinions of others, and finally start being who you want to be. . . . Although growing old disgracefully is a skill that can be learned at any age, you would have to want to do it enough to take the risks . . . it's a way of life that grows from the contradictions in women's experiences, from the antagonism between our curious and life-affirming core, and our socialization as women. It grows from every small, subversive act and every strategy we've used to help us survive. It is already there in those rare moments when, like weeds poking through cracks in the concrete, we give the world a glimpse of an authentic person who refuses to play by all the patriarchal rules. It is there, waiting to be released from pretense.

Commenting on bookshelves currently overflowing with advice on "aging gracefully," medical writer Robin Marantz Henig, in a review of *Ourselves, Growing Older: Women Aging with Knowledge and Power* (1988, p. 4), insists that "Grace isn't the point here. Strength is, individuality is, feistiness is."

An old age I had the fortune to observe was that of my husband's mother who lived the last decade of her 96 years in a comfortable apartment attached to the home of her oldest son and his wife. Grandma Katy lived into old age fed, tended, soothed, listened to, talked with, sat with, combed, dressed, joked with and cared for with enormous love and respect by two generations of two large families. I am grateful for and in awe of this big, rural German family that took good care of her. Few old women today have the option of aging and dying in such a supportive atmosphere.

Always herself in both German communities she lived in, Katy played the harmonica for many years. The last time we were with her, the visit of a family of musicians led one granddaughter to bring Katy's harmonica to the bedside. We were the audience for her last concert, this tiny old woman summoning up enough breath to play one song on her mouthharp, the air around her body and bed glowing with her spirit, her family's devotion, and our unbridled joy at this serendipitous moment.

Of Caroline Preston, a founder of the Seattle Older Woman's League, and professor at the University of Washington Department of Psychiatry and Behavioral Sciences, Joan Gaines (1987, p. 7) wrote that "she helped debunk many of the myths of old age and initiated a program to introduce medical students to facts about aging. Shortly before she died [May 7, 1987], she felt that the 'dark side' of growing old also needed to be expressed." Preston (1987) wrote:

Lately I have been hearing a new theme song for the elderly. A folder for long-term health insurance shows older men and women engaged in all kinds of activities; however worthy, these are improbable or unlikely. . . . Such optimistic views of aging are as hard on us as our previous invisibility. We find ourselves yearning to be like people in these pictures and belabor ourselves for failing these role models.

As I age, I marvel we do as well as we do. The erosion of autonomy in aging is incessant. . . . Making plans was always a joy to me. . . . Now I am chary about committing myself to plans of any kind. Rarely bored earlier, I am often sick of my sick self. The illnesses of old age are like exotic birds. We have maladies no one can account for. . . . Often friends may comment on our apparent good mood (and) this can become a mandate to be cheerful at all costs lest we disappoint our well-meaning friends.

Ageism is especially difficult to confront and change if one is not aware of one's own internalized ageism. I silently rail at other drivers and feel justified in my criticism when I see the driver is old. Not wanting to be called old myself, I project that distinction on another and quickly realize I must nurture the courtesy and compassion in me that I want myself. I cringed, walking one morning over a land bridge, to hear two little boys derisively yelling "Grandma!" up at me. Where did they learn to make fun of gray-haired people, I wondered?

I catch myself making bad jokes about both thermostats and the television sound turned up high in the rooms of old people. And many of us make a joke about Alzheimer's disease when we cannot remember something.

Aunt Caroline does not bother anyone any more, living in that nursing home, at age 102 receiving greetings from politicians honoring her age. In fact, "aging gracefully" may mean simply not causing anyone any trouble. She may be all those things the women thought of to describe "aging gracefully." Yet she is also old, probably tired, eating very little, sleeping lots, smiling or staring at her caretakers, surrounded by other old people and probably remembering the years of her earlier life.

"The real archetypal image, then, would be the foolish old man and the foolish old woman," says psychiatrist and Jungian therapist Adolf Guggenbuhl-Craig in a letter announcing a seminar at the New York C. G. Jung Foundation titled "Aging: Old Bottles, New Wine." He goes on:

> Their wisdom would lie in allowing themselves to be beyond all the conventions and expectations of their surroundings and not care, to freely show their deficiencies, to admit that they 'don't understand the world anymore' but enjoy living all the same, and to cease in the quest for power. They would be liberated from the coercions of collective life, free of the compulsion to do the right thing and (free of the compulsion) to be intelligent and wise. In this freedom the archetypal meaning of old age finally would be discovered by everyone.

Is old age a time of freedom or conformity? Do women have choices? Have we exercised these choices before we are old? Surely we can be less demanding of ourselves and our sisters, less demanding that we maintain our culture's requirements, more willing to widen our own horizons of aging, of behavior, of appearance. We can learn not to criticize and judge each other, can be more willing to embrace our differences and to enlarge our ability to accept one another. Marcy Adelman, editor of *Long Time Passing: Lives of Older Lesbians* and feminist therapist, says: ". . . If you're not accepting of yourself at any age, it makes sense that you're not going to be adjusting as well to whatever stage or period you're in" (1987, p. 7).

Carl Jung once defined love as giving the other the benefit of the doubt. Grace is neither perfectionism, nor not bothering another. "Aging gracefully" means being "full of grace," not that which is bestowed by some heavenly deity but grown and nurtured and developed from within ourselves and from our communities; that which enlarges and strengthens and empowers one's aging. This last and significant passage of my life, my aging, deserves my full attention and devotion. *Yes!*

Chapter 4

LOOKS

In twentieth century American culture, women are encouraged from every quarter to choose a different "master" than one's self, the most insidious of which says we are to go to any length — even that of having our bodies cut up and rearranged — to look young, even though that look is often produced under false standards of health or beauty, and against our own choice.

I do not suggest there is a standard for every woman. I let my hair grow out to its natural gray from the light brown I maintained for years with dye, and yet it is a source of continual embarrassment to me that, at my age, I worry about my LOOKS. Yet I understand and respect the wisdom of another aging woman, a psychology professor in a large university, who kept her hair dyed a soft blond in order to keep people in her department from treating her like an old woman, examples of which she knew well.

I am not talking about general conformity to dress and appearance codes of our culture — norms such as men rarely wearing skirts, although women may wear pants; babies being naked in front of others; certain special occasions requiring fancier than normal clothing; or clothing changes with the seasons, first born out of necessity. (One of American culture's oddities is that we have topless bars, yet most people avert their eyes from mothers nursing their babies in public!)

What I am talking about are dress and appearance codes — sometimes called "Looks-ism" — that have nothing to do with necessity and everything to do with vanity and how others view us.

Old women become invisible, nonsexual, and seldom exhibit what is considered a nice appearance by the media. Sociologist

Becky Thompson, in an article titled "Women's Hunger and Feeding Ourselves," tells us about

> an eleven billion dollar reducing industry in which 95% of the consumers are women; a medical system which maintains the dubious assumption that fat is by definition unhealthy and needs to be eliminated; a multi-billion dollar advertising industry which markets a race, class and age-biased model of beauty; a job market in which women who do not fit this model of beauty must deal with discrimination; as well as an insurance industry that penalizes those who do not maintain the medically prescribed image of what constitutes a healthy body size. (1988, p. 78)

Magazines and television, even in the programs and issues directed to the "elderly" market, show women who are young or barely middle-aged, as thin, apparently financially secure, confident, beautifully coiffed and dressed, extroverted, attractive-to-men, and heterosexually-coupled. Daily, the aging woman has opportunities to feel insecure, out of fashion, undesirable, fat, unattractive, sexless, pathetic, and unable from any standpoint to find or maintain the image of beauty, even aging beauty if in fact there is such a thing.

Social scientist and researcher Jean Kilbourne brilliantly shows what advertising does to women, including old women, in two half-hour videos titled "Killing Us Softly" and "Still Killing Us Softly." Kilbourne details specific ads, pointing out the violent, misogynist, hierarchical, sexist use of women in mainstream marketing. Revealing how women are used to sell the socially-acceptable drug alcohol, "Calling the Shots" is another of Kilbourne's startling video presentations; which details much about the sexism and ageism rampant in American culture (1982).

Even as old people become a large, important segment of the population, and longer lives cause marketers to cater to the aging population, the real truth still lies hidden under the slick pages of magazines and beyond the constant images of the television screen.

Reality is not the advertiser's intent; to encourage people to buy their product is. That undeniable fact makes sense. The problem is that most women almost unconsciously accept these images as reality and thus feel bad about themselves, and strive to emulate something that is not true or valid for their lives.

Advertisers might also represent the reverse of our nation's shadow—the fear of death, the fear of the power of old women, reflecting the national need to deny anything which is unpleasant or causes turmoil or pain. The cult of youth, positivism, individualism, of insisting that we are the good guys, and never harboring a dark instinct—all deeply-ingrained habits and attitudes—contribute to the denigration and invisibility of aging women.

Speaking to the 1987 West Coast Old Lesbian Conference and Celebration, writer and old woman Barbara Macdonald asks bluntly:

What is it then that we dread? Is it not some unnamed fear of the future, something that keeps moving ahead of us but is never where we are? Are we not dealing with a myth of old age, an accumulated deposit of everyone's fears of the uncertainty of life, which all of society has pushed ahead each year until it is compressed into the farthest end of our lives? Then we, who are old, are expected to live out everyone's fear, not of old age, but . . . of the uncertainty of life itself.

Oppressions are uncovered by only one group—those who daily feel the oppression, whose lives are chipped away by each encounter until one day, one woman, and then another, decides, 'No more. I will not ignore this hatred . . . whether it is disguised as deference, honor, respect, or sympathy, or presents itself as naked hatred of my aging body or as a primitive fear of my old and ancient rage. . . .' Age is a time of great wonder—a time when we have to hold, with a fine balance, contradictory truths in our heads and give them equal weight. Old is scary but very exciting, chaotic but self-integrating; narrowing yet wider; weaker yet stronger than ever before. It is we who must name the processes of our own aging . . . we cannot explore our aging without examining and confronting ageism. It is the task that lies before us." (pp. 3, 15)

The difficulties of adolescence and growing up do not foster appreciation of and respect for our bodies, nor is there much teaching to value our physical self. The physical body is expected to conform to some external ideal. Religious systems tell us a future heaven is more important than this life and that spirit is more important than matter, anything more significant than our material body. Ernest Becker in *The Denial of Death* (1973) describes our species as ashamed and embarrassed to be so human as to have to put up with daily bodily functions.

Old women are benevolently called "grandmother," an overt reminder that one has borne children and is still in the caretaking role. A few favored women become famous for something and are then thought to be wise, the other suitable role for old women. One must be useful! When no longer sexually useful, or involved in taking care of others, we are encouraged to hide who we are, to feel good about ourselves with dyes, surgery, cosmetics, makeup, clothes and strenuous exercise. To claim one's "oldness" in a culture that tells us to deny that reality puts women in a double bind. Is it any wonder that depression, feelings of uselessness, and low self-esteem are so well-known to the aging woman!

"There is a tendency in our community (lesbian)," Marcy Adelman (Charland 1987, p. 8) reports, "just as there is outside in the mainstream, to see old women as sexless. We neuterize them. The other thing is seeing old women as mothers. That's another way of objectifying them . . . rather than that these are women we can enter into reciprocal relationships with, whole people in other words."

So we pass for younger than we are. At least most women appear to be doing so. A common thrilling compliment is "You don't look your age" or "I can't tell who is the mother and who the daughter." "I would never have guessed your age" tells us we still belong, are viewed as attractive, have not yet been relegated to the trash heap of women who are no longer useful because their appearance isn't young enough, pretty enough, thin enough, fashionable enough, or sexy enough.

Aphorisms such as "You're as young as you feel," "Age is just a state of mind," and "growing young" constantly feed the well-entrenched attitude that old is bad, ugly, to be avoided, wrong, preventable, or shameful. Our culture says there is a fountain of youth and we get in line at the drinking fountain every day. My friend and preacher Gordon Cosby, of the Church of the Savior,

Washington, D.C., says we are like alcoholics who take 10 to 15 drinks of our culture every day and think we can stay sober.

Aging and trying to look young at the same time are a Catch-22 for many women. We often say, "She certainly doesn't act her age," or "That outfit is too young for her. Who does she think she is?" and "That woman looks so artificial with that . . . (wig, makeup, dyed hair, young-looking clothes, brittle smile, etc.)."

I also do and say such things. I cringed for Lucille Ball at her last national TV appearance, dyed, heavily made-up, and simpering beside the male host. On a short trip last spring, I stopped for lunch and became fascinated by eight women playing bridge in the corner of the restaurant. As they came by my table on their way to the restroom, I observed that they were all rail thin, heavily made-up, had dyed hair, wore high-heeled shoes in which they took mincing steps, and were all clothed in Ultrasuede. I was caught both criticizing and feeling sorry for them, as they presented themselves in the only way their culture told them was attractive. Where was my compassion for these women, my feelings of solidarity with my sisters?

How can we dress to please ourselves? (I do not advocate rudeness or insensitivity to other cultures nor to those we respect within our own. The uncomfortable memory lingers that I wore my white middle-class leisure clothes — denim skirt and dress-up T-shirt — to a Winnebago Powwow one year, and heard later from a friend's mother that the Native American women were offended by my casual attire at a ceremony to which they wear their finest traditional clothes.) How do we begin to free ourselves from the huge amounts of money and effort it takes to live up to someone else's idea of beauty or appropriateness? How can we free ourselves from the multi-billion dollar industries that tell us what to weigh, how to look, what to wear, how to be healthy (according to someone's vested interest), how to be employed and considered useful?

Around the whole issue of what our bodies look like, an excellent manual for change is Susan Kano's *Making Peace With Food: Freeing Yourself from the Diet/Weight Obsession* (1989). I cannot recommend it highly enough. Dr. Mary Pipher's fine book *Hunger Pains: The American Women's Tragic Quest for Thinness* (1988), focuses on her work with anorexic and bulimic women and is an excellent source for women wanting to free themselves from this national addiction.

Some things I try to do, or not do, include: not watching television; not weighing myself, even though I am constantly tempted and sometimes succumb in the locker room of the pool where I swim; never, ever again going on a diet; actively pursuing images of larger women; responding to remarks about someone's "nice figure" with questions about what constitutes a "nice figure." With my youngest daughter Amy, I had the empowering experience last winter of spending women's night at a bathhouse in Denver, one of only a handful still in existence in this country, naked and comfortable with bodies of all shapes and sizes and women of all ages. The sauna, steam room, whirlpools, benches and showers were full of women chatting, comfortable with themselves for a few hours, relieved of the need to look "good," whatever that awful and disabling dictum means. Humorist Erma Bombeck asked in a recent column on cultural appearance requirements for women: "When does it stop? Isn't there ever a time when we can accept the principle of gravity and get on with our lives?"

As the advertisements do not say, look how far we have to go! We have miles to go to reclaim our true selves from the media, from industries that make money by telling us we are not okay, from the constricting stereotypes of patriarchal models and institutions, and their fear of old women. How we need to reflect to ourselves and other old women our worth and beauty!

Black is beautiful.
Old is beautiful.
Fat is beautiful.
Who we are is beautiful.
Beauty is in the eye of the beholder and the eye is our own.

Chapter 5

Call It by Its Name

Language says a lot about what we believe. To call someone "old" is to criticize, to give her or him a bad name. Think of the words substituted for "old": elderly, senior citizen, golden ager, mature, advanced, distinguished, silver-haired. (There are not as many synonyms for old as for two other conditions we also find difficult to face: "dead" and "drunk" lead the list of words with the most euphemisms.)

The word "old" is reserved for anyone older than we are — parents when we are children, really old people (beyond 40) when we are first grown-up, or *really* old people (of 60) when we reach our thirties. As old woman writer Barbara Macdonald (1987) explains, we keep pushing our fears of aging on to some age beyond our own, thinking that at some later age we will be old. We usually consider only someone older than ourselves, even if we're 90, to be truly old.

"Gerontological literature typically starts it (older) at 65-75, which is considered 'young old,' 75 up is considered 'old old,'" Marcy Adelman (Charland 1987, p. 1) reports in an interview with *Bay Windows*, New England's largest gay and lesbian newspaper. "65 probably has to do with economics around social security. We need to understand that these are all political categories."

"Old is equated with 'awful' in every respect, with regard to function, thought, action, appearance," writes Shevy Healey, feminist psychotherapist. "I mentioned the Older Women's League (OWL) to a friend and her instant response was, 'What an awful name!'" (Healey 1986, p. 58)

I, too, am counseled by a good friend to change the name of the course I teach from "Women and Aging: Celebrating Ourselves" to something more attractive to women, so that they don't have to categorize themselves as "aging." Few women in this society are willing to call themselves "old" at sixty-six, as Baba Copper did in order to "escape the prissy category of *older woman*" (Copper 1986, p. 47).

People speak euphemistically in order not to shock, to be polite, to evade a harsh reality, to avoid hard-to-feel emotions, to give a hazy gloss to things which are unpleasant, uncomfortable, or which can leave one feeling powerless. Viewing Aunt Emma's body at the funeral parlor we say to one another, "Doesn't she look lovely?" and find fault with doctors and hospitals, often scapegoating them for our unwillingness to accept that a loved one is dying. We sing hymns and listen to prayers about a dead person "being on the other side," "passing away," and "going to her reward," to comfort ourselves when a life has ended. At the other extreme of expression, a nuclear submarine was once named "Corpus Christi," Latin for the "body of Christ." We often name in order to evade or prevent knowing.

Many scoff at the feminist movement's insistence on inclusive language, hiding their own disagreement with equal opportunity under arguments about the gender-neutrality of the male pronoun. As Gracia Fay Ellwood, a religious studies teacher at California State University at Long Beach writes, "We cannot so easily disclaim responsibility for the semi-conscious effects of our language on others (and ourselves)" (1988, p. 28).

In a powerful and revealing treatise on "Women, Language, and Power," presented in 1990 at the Unitarian Church, Lincoln, NE, Dr. Sally Stoddard provided numerous examples of how current language controls our own and other people's lives. She examined news stories, advertisements and current language usage to make the relationship between power and language clear, suggesting that becoming aware of one's own usage and that of others leads us a long way toward "the power to control, at the least, our own lives."

In *When Society Becomes An Addict,* (1987) Anne Wilson Schaef reminds us:

In her book, *The Wizard of Earthsea,* Ursula LeGuin describes how to become a wizard. During the lengthy process of training and education, it is necessary to spend a concentrated block of time with the Master Namer, a teacher who knows the *true* name for everything. The true name is different from the common, public name. When you learn the true name of something, you are able to take back any power it has over you. We need to do that with the system in which we live.

In her book *Silences* (1987, p. 10), Tillie Olsen points out how our refusal to speak our reality or name our experiences makes us accomplices of a system that oppresses us. Only by naming can we reclaim our reality and our power.

Part of becoming old is to call things by their accurate names. Dying is dying, dead is dead, old is old. Many synonyms and euphemisms describe and refer to conditions of death and aging; I must first name such conditions accurately in order not to lose track of the reality they stand for. I am not advocating being rude by using language a particular group considers bad form; in a group of people who say "passed" for "died," one might want to adopt such a custom. "When in Rome" is often good advice. Listening to what words mean to another is social compassion. However, unlike so many cultures which *do not* evade and avoid the reality of death, old age or what our Puritan ethic considers the grossness of being human, we isolate ourselves from real feelings, the truth of things, and from the power that comes with acceptance.

We can find, along with the late (another euphemism?) Baba Copper, that "Younger is not better, it is simply different. Embracing one's years means that old is good." We must stop "erasing any image of our own future" by claiming the last third of our lives. To separate aging and ageism, Copper defines: "Aging is a real process which takes place differently in each individual. Ageism is a constriction that rearranges power relationships (in which) one is shaped into something that is always less than what one really is" (Copper 1986, p. 47).

It is a real cause of celebration if women can manage to extricate themselves from the messages that say that old is ugly, awful, and to be avoided at all costs. In Healey's words, it means to be myself . . . to deal with what is different, special, unique about being older . . . to learn to live with loss and death, to prepare for my own death . . . to attend to the current business of living with vigor and involvement while at the same time attending to the unfinished business of my life, putting old rancors in perspective, letting go of pettiness, acknowledging love. (Healey 1986, p. 62)

Chapter 6

Just Try Harder

This morning I had a wrestling match with that person inside me who constantly insists that I "try harder." I suspect it is my workaholic self that can never be satisfied. Its voice tells me that I play-pretend to be a responsible, functioning, grown-up person, and that my attempts to find meaning and purpose in what I do — writing, teaching and social justice work — are ludicrous.

Is it generic to women to doubt ourselves, or an affliction of women of my generation to think of ourselves as second-class as long as we are not being paid much or at all for our efforts? This reflection does not focus on the two-career family, or on the problems of the woman who has been tricked into thinking she can be mother, wage earner, companion and sane at the same time. That is a real issue but not the one I am facing today.

Each day I anxiously move into my work, "anxiously" being the key word. It is as if I must hurry, force myself to work, justify myself or fall back into sloth and dependence, or be called lazy by inner voices, the penalty for not responding to those inner imperatives.

The siren, or judging voice tells me I must earn money for my work (enormously important for women, both to support one's self, to be financially independent, and to receive just compensation for one's energies); I must do something significant, interact with other people and people from the world of commerce and power. All these "musts" then justify my use of time.

I have such a powerful inner demand for outer performance and little tolerance for unscheduled time! During an annual weekend in Florida for a board meeting, I cringe at the sight of old couples wandering around, looking for ways to fill their days or for something to be interested in. This might be a projection of my fear of aging.

Activities to which I attach no importance leave me in panic. I used to play bridge with a group of women who led busy social lives, and among other talents, were expert at decorating their homes, choosing beautiful clothing for themselves and their children, things that have never been easy for me. At nearly every meeting I screamed at myself, "What in god's name am I doing here?"

Now I carefully choose things to do that match some inner wisdom and a hard-won value system. My tendency to be self-righteous is tempered by the memory of something asked of me during inpatient treatment for recovery from alcoholism several years ago. I was asked to join the card games in the day room, which I hated, at which I was not adept, and over which I felt embarrassment. Was the idea to make me socialize, to practice doing nothing, to do something I considered a waste of time, did not enjoy and I did not excel at, or to do something that didn't matter? A dear old friend and therapist, Olga, once told me I was a "D" running around acting like an "A." I did not ask what a "D" personality was, perhaps afraid of the answer.

Still, I continue to justify much of my activity and behavior, knowing that rationalization hides another agenda. As I keep terribly busy in order not to feel bad, I ignore advice from friends who say that to do nothing or to have unscheduled time is a way of honoring and making a connection with one's deepest self. Writer May Sarton uses the powerful image of a lawn sprinkler, turning endlessly, the water from its source long depleted by constant motion.

I give lip service to the need for "being" as opposed to "doing," and honor introversion as the essential other side of our culture's extroversion. In a place inside myself, I know that vital psychic work is done by people in monasteries, prisons, and madhouses, acting out that side which is beyond the rational and functional. By confining people, we can avoid facing our own darkness. I can hide in my work, unlike people in institutions, and not break the law, become a monk or lose hold of my sanity. I can work relentlessly and pretend I do not pay an awful price.

I struggle, some days, to hold together my inner self, the terrible need to do meaningful work as opposed to the need to do nothing, and the need to be among others versus the need to be alone inside my house and myself when I write. On the days when these opposing forces get wildly out of balance, I try to find a semblance of peace by naming them, bringing the tension to consciousness and talking it out. This too, then, becomes my work.

As an aging woman, I must give myself permission to be who I am, even if that is not culturally approved or productive. I need time to be tired, quiet, sick, sad, old, and unproductive. I want to affirm who I am at each moment of my life, not wishing for another time, another self, nor molding myself to fit an inner shape that no longer serves.

(Since writing this chapter, I have made progress in talking back to that voice that condemns me, in finding more balance between my inner and outer life, and knowing, finally, the value of listening to what my body is telling me and following that. The learning and experience came, in part and in a profound way, from a week spent in a group of women with psychiatrist and author Jean Shimoda Bolen, and musician and dancer Jan Lovett-Keen, exploring "Women's Wisdom, the Sacred Feminine," at the Feathered Pipe Ranch in Montana.)

Chapter 7

Women's Work

What is Women's Work, I wonder, and what is the challenge to aging women found in their work? Is it to increase the world's consciousness? Is it to bring men to consciousness or to become like men in the workplace? Is it to work towards a matrilinear, matrifocal society? Is it to nurture others, to be the caretakers, to emphasize the right-brained poet in our souls, to redress the imbalance of the left-brained rational, productive personality so ascendant today?

Are women supposed to take care of, clean up after, or straighten out problems among others, or do they perform the meditative, reflective, monastic work of this wildly extroverted, linear society? Are women the ones to insist on truth-telling, to stop war and refuse to raise sons or daughters to be cannon fodder? Are we to continue to support male leaders while they dominate others and this planet? Are we called to give up our mite of the power structure in order to withdraw support from the dominance model of human society?

Several years ago I keynoted a YWCA program honoring "working women," which I believe includes all women. Generously borrowing from the experiences and writing of other women, I said:

Women have always worked . . . because they had to. . . .

Women everywhere have matter-of-factly taken on the necessary labor of survival and subsistence — child-bearing, family-caring, field-tending, wage-earning. . . . What is new is that women are *choosing* to work and that the work they are choosing to do is not justified solely by its contribution to the well-being of their families . . . claiming the right to do signif-

33

icant work raises the even larger issue of the place of meaningful work in adult life for all of us.

For women as for men generative activity includes creative,
productive work in one's own right as well as on behalf of
others, in the world as well as in the home. . . . (These essays
are) resonant with a human need to make a difference, to make
one's mark in the world by producing with dignity something
of use to others.

In a patriarchal world, female aspiration toward autono-
mous creative work is all too often dismissed, even deni-
grated, while women's initiative and competence outside the
home are perceived as threatening anomalies. . . . Our work
seems insufficiently hard or professional; if unpaid, it is somehow not serious — mere poetry. In the face of pervasive regard
for the "masculine," as well as the careerism and sheer com-
mercialism that continuously prejudice our judgments of human worth, we have had to learn to recognize and accept and
respect the authenticity and purpose in our work. . . . We who
have begun to work with confidence and pleasure do not ignore those whose work provides them with little pleasure or
purpose of any kind. (Ruddick and Daniels 1977, pp. xxv-
xxx)

In the same collection, Kay Keeshan Hamod writes in her essay,
"Finding New Forms":

Feminism does not speak for all women until it is able to push
for radical solutions to the problems that make it difficult for
many to survive, much less think about self-fulfillment. . . . I
must be able to communicate my expectations: that work be
socially valuable, as well as personally rewarding; that work
advance the process of self-discovery, revealing what we are
capable of doing and making; and that it should leave us with a
sense of integrity rather than shattering us physically and emotionally. (Ruddick and Daniels, 1977, p. 3)

In the foreword to *Working It Out* entitled, "Conditions for
Work: The Common World of Women," Adrienne Rich says:

> We had better face the fact that our hope . . . depends on
> seeking and giving our allegiance to a community of women
> (co-workers). This is not a question of generosity . . . that
> makes women in community support and nourish each other.
> It is rather what Whitman called the "hunger for equals."
> (1977, p. xiv)

For centuries women have been deeply involved in the work of
their communities, in farming, house-raising, teaching, preaching,
doctoring, running stores and businesses. At some point an idle
woman became a male status symbol and was thereby kept isolated
from interactions with others not controlled by her husband. This
change in women's status and power in the United States began
roughly in the last half of the 19th century. The return of men from
World War II further precipitated a movement of women to the
home after war work, to take care of children and men. Wage-
earning and going about in the workplace was reserved for men or
for those women not "fortunate" enough to be connected to a
wage-earning man.

In the last third of this century, women have entered the work
force outside the home again, for economic, psychological and
equalitarian reasons. These women struggle with gender inequality
in their positions, wages, power and influence, and with their own
desire and society's demand that they be superwomen in order to
succeed and be appreciated as women. Ruddick and Daniels (1987,
p. XXIX) know that: raised consciousness, whatever its ultimate
value, has brought vulnerability, invited risk and insisted on
change. Again Rich (1977, p. xvii) writes:

> For, in trying to join the common world of men, we split our-
> selves off from the common life of women and deny our fe-
> male heritage and identity in our work, we lose touch with our
> real powers and with the essential condition for all fully real-
> ized work: community.

In this same vein, Patricia Reis (1988, p. 82), an artist and wom-
en's therapist for the Women to Women clinic in Yarmouth, Maine
writes:

This is . . . foremost a woman's task . . . (to) meet the Dark Goddess first. Only when we have made the journey, have opened the passageway to those abandoned, rejected aspects of female energy in ourselves will we be able to come fully into our own inner power and bring ourselves deeply into creative relationship with another.

As we age, can we find another standard for our worth other than that of money paid, attention and influence gained, or universal acclaim for taking care of others? Is our worth simply that of being old? Is our success as old women based on having done our *work* of forgiveness, of living intentionally and consciously? Does the old woman have to have lived her life in a certain way in order to be respected in her old age? Is there some *work* she still must do? Can she give up singing for her supper, proving her worth, her mettle?

Is the work of our old age that of a new life? This point is beautifully chronicled by Carolyn Heilbrun in *Writing a Woman's Life*. She warns:

For women who have awakened to new possibilities in middle age, or who were born into the current women's movement and have escaped the usual rhythms of the once-traditional female existence, the last third of life is likely to require new attitudes and new courage. (1988, p. 124)

Heilbrun feels certain the changed life will be marked by laughter, and with that, the end of fantasy and daydreaming. She reflects on "the delusion of a passive life . . . the possibility of something being over, settled, sweeping clear the way for contentment" and shows us that "When the hope for closure is abandoned, when there is an end to fantasy, adventure for women will begin." The coming of age portends "all the freedoms men have always known and women never — mostly the freedom from fulfilling the needs of others and from being a female impersonator" (p. 130).

Sara Ruddick writes in "A Work of One's Own," in *Working It Out* (1977, p. 128),

At long last I have been *learning* to work. By that I mean that there is in my daily life a satisfactory predominance of activity over passivity, of reality over fantasy, of creation over conception. It continues to astonish me that this simple human ability to work brings so much additional pleasure, order, solace, and meaning to my life. . . . I needed to recover the inseparability of work and love common among children, natural to me as a schoolgirl . . . the loves that work demands in its own name: love for oneself, love for the ideas and creations of others, love for the people one works with, love for the knowledge, change, and beauty that work alone can achieve.

My friend Margaret and I talked recently about the energy that primary relationships demand. She is withdrawing from "working on" her partnership in order to do her work—on her projections, her dark side, the hidden corners, the Margaret inside.

I recently read, in a paper of a sister community of The Church of the Savior in the Adams-Morgan neighborhood in Washington, D.C., the following:

Every inward work requires an outward expression or it comes to nothing. In fact, it may even fracture us further, widening the split between what we subscribe to inwardly and what we do outwardly. This is why a person's work is always of utmost importance (in this instance, what one does in the outer, physical world). "Being" and "doing" complete each other . . . . We cannot choose one above the other without falling into great trouble.

What is my work in this lifetime? Is it to create? To learn patience? To speak my truth? To earn a living? To help others? To do the dailyness without wondering what is my work?

Old age increases the insistence of these questions. Perhaps one of the requirements of aging is to find the time and energy to pursue whatever one's work is, to claim as work both the roots growing in dark, deep soil, and the flowering in the daylight; the searching roots and the answering blossoms.

II. ANGER, HURT, GRIEF, AND CHANGE: FACING OURSELVES

Chapter 8

Who Am I Going To Be When I Grow Up?

Remember the book, *I'm Running Away from Home but I'm Not Allowed to Cross the Street: A Primer of Women's Liberation* (Burton, 1972)? It is a story of a woman and her marriage, her children, her role as helper to her husband and manager of their household and social life. She leaves that milieu, midstream as it were, barely managing to survive outside and beyond that traditional woman's role.

I read that book in the late 1970s, a time of growth for me. My idea of adult life, until then, consisted of marrying, having children, being part of a couple, deriving my power from a male partner, and keeping house as my mother did before me.

During those sometimes painful midlife years between the ages of 30 and 50, my friends and I said to one another somewhat facetiously, "I wonder who I'll be when I grow up." For those of us not defined by career or vocation, we thought a time would come when we would be someone else, not entirely wife and mother. We had little idea of who that person might be. Even women with a vocational definition — teacher, farmer, lawyer, writer, bookkeeper, paid or not — at some point may find that they are operating out of someone else's values, not having clearly defined their own.

However faint it sounded, I heard a call that has become loud and insistent in this last third of my life, actually a demand that I grow beyond my dependent, role-bound and defined self.

Anthropologist Ashley Montagu insists in *Growing Young* (1981) that "we were never intended to 'grow up' into the kind of adults most of us have become," the ossified adults prescribed by society.

In his description of neoteny, the process of growing young,

Montagu makes clear that the idea of becoming adult, mature or growing-up—especially ignored in the culturally-demanded hurry to become a heterosexual couple—not only is wrong, but stultifying. The young race after the power and freedom they perceive in adults, yearn to grow up faster, wish to be like the adults living 'real' life, beyond that of childhood.

Montagu demonstrates how our culture, schools, and families are in conspiracy against childlike traits, all those qualities with which the child is so abundantly and favorably endowed:

> Those traits of childhood behavior that are so valuable and that tend to disappear gradually as human beings grow older . . . [including] curiosity, imaginativeness, playfulness, open-mindedness, willingness to experiment, flexibility, humor, energy, receptiveness to new ideas, honesty, eagerness to learn, the need to love. (p. 2)

"Children ask questions endlessly," Montagu observes. "They can keep themselves busy for hours with the simplest toys . . . play games endlessly . . . accept changes without defensiveness . . . they laugh. Unless they suspect they may be punished for it, they tell the truth . . . they soak up knowledge and information like sponges."

Words, written by psychiatrist Thomas Szasz (1977, p. 21-22), posted on my bulletin board for years, remind that:

> Every act of conscious learning requires the willingness to suffer an injury to one's self esteem. That is why young children, before they are aware of their own self importance, learn so easily and why older persons, especially if vain or self important have great difficulty learning at all—pride and vanity can thus be greater obstacles to learning than stupidity.

A large body of scientific research and reflection makes clear that the truth about the human species is that in body, spirit, feeling, and conduct we are designed to grow and develop in ways that *emphasize* rather than minimize childlike traits.

Montagu (1981, p. 4) traces the history of valuing being old or young. "In Western industrialized, and to some extent in even not-so-affluent other parts of the world, the cult of youth has come to be a kind of secular religion . . . and given rise to and also a result of a multibillion-dollar industry.'' (Not that the cult of youth values the growth and development of children as described by Montagu, concentrating, as it does almost entirely, on the physical characteristics of being young).

> Such worship of youth was not always in vogue. Until some time after World War II, in Britain and Western Europe as well as in the United States, to be old was revered. Governments were run by graybeards, the world's business was conducted by old men and families were subject to the wills of their oldest members.
>
> Women, of course, suffered under this regime even more than men, because daughters were considered even more immature, more vulnerable, and more dependent than sons, and in greater need of supervision and protection. Childhood was seen as a difficult period that was unfortunately necessary for the production of mature, no-nonsense adults . . . the closer their behavior to that of adults, the better. (Montagu, p. 5)

"We have made some progress in this understanding over the past 50 years," Montagu reports. Many scientists and educators "have begun to recognize that children are not simply small imperfect adults who must be dragged as early as possible into the adult-behaving world.''

Montagu (1981, p. 6) reports that research begun by zoologist Julius Kollman in 1884, and continued by scientists Havelock Ellis, Louise Bolk, J.B.S. Haldan, and Konrad Lorenz, led "directly to a belief that human beings are designed to retain into adulthood many of the behavioral traits that characterize human childhood.'' This is such a Catch-22, or -44, that women are caught in, because of our need to grow up, in a healthy way, before we get old!

To be serious, sober adults leaves out the very characteristics that allow us to grow, change and develop. Montagu adds that German sociologist Arnold Gehlen recognized as early as 1940 that the unique and outstanding human trait is that of remaining in an unending state of development . . . the specialty of humans is nonspecialization, versatility; they have remained free to change as change is required by whatever environment they encounter. (p. 8)

Growing up in a linear, duality-dominated patriarchy, our lives appear to go in a line from birth to death, not in a circular, spiral process. We are accustomed to separate, label and make judgments about life and death, young and old, good and bad, productive and lazy, heaven and hell, bodies versus minds, black and white, and feeling versus thinking, in an effort not only to make sense of this short span of time but to control and manage it. We often try to define it in ways that allow us to "grow up," to be like those whose power and possessions we envy.

For old women, or women becoming old, the charge is to "grow up" in middle age, and to "grow up" into a value system that honors their lives, their years, their age, their bodies and to be careful of all sisters and brothers. This process allows one to shed the false values of the culture and traditional thought patterns of "growing up," validate and affirm one's true self, shed the preoccupation with conforming, with power over, and with contorting one's self in order to belong, to be noticed and to be approved.

Theologian Ann Belford Ulanov (1986, p. 66) describes the journey thus:

If we spend a lifetime avoiding who we are, veering off from the central issues of finding and building our personal way of being, our personal ways of putting ourselves into the world; of facing the hard questions of injustice and suffering — or the sometimes harder ones of justice and pleasure — of facing the blasting challenges of really loving someone more than ourselves; of surviving failure and learning from it; of reaching to the center, always the center, seeing persons as uniquely themselves, not fully defined by class or economic level or education or talent, we reap the results in old age. We survive as unique persons who go on growing, experiencing, changing, and consolidating ourselves. Life continues to offer excitement.

According to an old saying, as we age, we become more of who we already are. Therefore it behooves me, to make sure that who I am is someone I like and want to be, someone whose life is satisfying and on the mark, before I am really old.

The truth of neoteny, and not a sentimental denial of aging, offers a challenge and opportunity to rediscover the qualities of our childlike selves, a way to stay open to life and all its possibilities right up to our last breath.

Chapter 9

Who Am I?

My friend, Nan, wrote to me one spring: "I know who I am and that is all I can be. Most days it's not much. But then, just to be myself . . . maybe that's enough." Both the surprise and the limitation of knowing who I am, after weathering the midlife transition, is a seminal issue for me in these years of becoming old and, I think, surely for other aging women.

For much of some women's lives, they have been who they thought they were supposed to be, who they imagined someone else wanted them to be, and who others told them to be. They internalized and increased all those messages by adding a version of their idealized self.

Awareness of mortality can send us deep into ourselves or into frenzied activity and/or deep depression, to do whatever it is we must do before we die. To discover that real woman under all those layers of socialization and expectation becomes the task.

In writing about what happens when "the myths that have driven our institutions are exposed," Madonna Kolbenschlag says in *Lost in the Land of Oz: The Search for Identity and Community in American Life* (1988, pp. 104-5):

> The project of the true self has been abandoned. Colonization is subtle. It is partly the fault of our own passivity and lack of vigilance, but it is also an inexorable effect of the systems that absorb us: family, workplace, class, gang or peer group, education, profession, and media. Each of these systems . . . becomes a ritual text that can estrange us from our real, true self. Instead we are left with a kind of laminated persona, each layer easily exploited by a culture in which many systems are in a runaway state.

Reclaiming our personal power, our sense of belonging to ourselves and to others as fellow human beings, requires that we challenge the myths of power that have shaped us. . . The first is our *faith in dominance and, consequently, hierarchy.* There are many subcorollaries . . . such as "men take charge," "father knows best," "heroes are loners." . . . The second is our *denial of our mortality and fallibility, of our finite capacity.* There are many subcorollaries to this myth also: the idolization of technology, denial of death in life, perfectionism, compulsive celebrity, "more is better," organization over organism.

I often say that I do not want to die having missed the point. Poet Marge Piercy writes in "If They Come in the Night," one of her selected poems in *Circles on the Water* (1982, pp. 222-23 [italics in second verse mine]),

Long ago on a night of danger and vigil
a friend said, *Why are you happy?*
He explained (we lay together
on a hard cold floor) what prison
meant because he had done
time, and I talked of the death
of friends. *Why are you happy*
then, he asked, close to
angry.

I said, I like my life. If I
have to give it back, if they
take it from me, let me only
not feel I wasted any, let me
not feel I forgot to love anyone
I meant to love, that I forgot
to give what I held in my hands,
that I forgot to do some little
piece of the work that wanted to come through.

Sun and moonshine, starshine,
the muted grey light off the waters
of the bay at night, the white

light of the fog stealing in,
the first spears of the morning
touching a face
I love. We all lose everything. We lose
ourselves. We are lost.

Only what we manage to do
lasts, what love sculps from us;
but what I count, my rubies, my
children, are those moments
wide open when I know clearly
who I am, who you are, what we
do, a marigold, an oakleaf, a meteor,
with all my senses hungry and filled
at once like a pitcher with light.

In *At Seventy, A Journal* (1984, p. 10), writer May Sarton answers the question: "Why is it good to be old? Because I am more
myself than I have ever been." One may not get "better" in the
conventional sense of the world — not look like a fashion plate or
have lots of answers. There may be confusion and ambivalence and
it is possible to become dismayed with the world and one's friends.

One may also speak one's own truth more often, say "no" to
things more easily and not waste energy tilting at the windmills of
fools quite so often. As my friend does, women may find their
limitations, a very plain sense of being enough or even some serenity with being "not much."

Writer and Jungian analyst Florida Scott-Maxwell says, in *The
Measure of My Days* (1979, p. 13),

Age puzzles me. I thought it was a quiet time. My seventies
were interesting, and fairly serene, but my eighties are passionate. I grow more intense as I age. To my own surprise I
burst out with hot conviction. Only a few years ago I enjoyed
my tranquility; now I am so disturbed by the outer world and
by human quality in general that I want to put things right, as
though I still owed a debt to life. I must calm down. I am far
too frail to indulge in moral fervor.

Later Scott-Maxwell (ibid, p. 42) says: "You need only claim the events of your life to make yourself yours. When you truly possess all you have been and done, which may take some time, you are fierce with reality."

Some women engage in discounting themselves, making fun of the woman who is "finding herself," internalizing the backlash against women who want more, seeking change, and upsetting the current "order." These women want more than what writer Carolyn Heilbrun (1988, Sept. 4) calls "loneliness at worst, golf at best." The outer furniture of a life — jobs, commitments, marriages, duties, old pleasures — may get rearranged and there may also be enormous inner turmoil that brings one closer to the bone of who one is.

Issues struggled with for years may lessen in importance or become worth the pain of change in order to resolve them. Issues such as dependence on a partner or children, general malaise about one's life, the need to focus and prioritize, to accept limitations, to push one's horizons, to become financially independent and/or more response/able, or to find what one truly loves and live out of that, all crack through the tough wall of overactivity or blast one out of the slough of despair.

This change may mean wearing different clothes, no longer putting on makeup, not going to certain events, finding joy in knowing someone we passed by before or no longer seeing an old friend. We might be less involved in day-to-day problems, emotional swings with family and friends or respond less quickly to the ringing of the telephone.

Inner work acts out in splendid variety and familiar patterns. Renowned therapist Karen Horney (1945, p. 240) wrote, "Fortunately analysis is not the only way to resolve inner conflicts. Life itself still remains a very effective therapist." She adds, though, that "Life as a therapist is ruthless."

My inner journey is not consistent nor always appropriate to my outer life. Listening to that inner voice *and* finding the courage to act upon it often differs from my traditional and typical responses to life and to others. It is hard to follow both communal norms and the inner call to selfhood. Sometimes I straddle the fence, jump back-

and-forth, and occasionally plunk down on one side or the other, with solitude, activity, or by following my schedule or intuition.

In this journey of the last third of life, I find that my grasp still exceeds my reach. Everyone faces their own issues in their own way; mine feels awkward, listening to what my body tells me, understanding the symbols offered in my dreams, and listening to people I trust.

I may have taken on too much when I announced to myself that I did not intend to spend the rest of my life complaining about my life or blaming others for my discomfort. My middle daughter Mary sent me a note years ago, which is taped to my desk blotter and now yellowed, that reminds me, in the words of one William J. Harris: "Neatness, madam, has nothing to do with the truth. The truth is quite messy—like a wind-blown room."

I do not know what aging will bring, this paring down and peeling away. It may not be something I do as much as something I observe, such as my ego becoming less rampant in the face of old age and death. (It may simply be, as Dr. Jonas Salk describes evolution to Arianna Stassinopoulas (1984, p. 10) in an article, getting up one more time than I fall down.)

There seem to be few blinding, instant, life-changing experiences on this journey, only a series of moments when I come closer to my true self—hints and whispers, some idea of the next step to take or gentle nudges. I feel some shame that this reflection is the luxury of a middle-class white woman born in the United States. I do not struggle for food and shelter or safety, as most women in Africa and Latin America do, and many even in the United States. One year I returned home from five hard, lonely weeks in Peru, knowing that I have to live the life I was born into and not be ashamed that I am not poor, or struggling to survive under desperate circumstances. Nor must I long to have been born someone else.

Again I turn to Ann Ulanov's (1986, p. 74) uncompromising words:

> Aging brings home to us what we have done or failed to do with our lives, our creativity or our waste, our openness or zealous hiding from what really matters. Precisely at that point, aging cracks us open, sometimes for the first time,

makes us aware of the center, makes us look for it and for relation to it. Aging does not mark an end but rather the beginning of making sense of the end-questions so that our life can have an end in every sense of the word.

I am aware of the many privileges in my life, one of which is to know better who I am as I age and the freedom to explore new ways of being. Such reflection on one's journey is not dependent on money, position, education or power, as stunningly demonstrated by artist Elizabeth Layton. In *Women and Aging: An Anthology by Women* (1986, p. 148), Lucy Lippard writes of Layton:

> In 1977, at age 68 . . . [she] saved her own life and added immeasurably to ours. The medium of salvation was large, colored-pencil drawings . . . the supplies bought at the drugstore in Wellsville, Kansas. . . . Her drawings are not only "high quality," but offer a view of American life rarely reflected in contemporary art. Aging, depression, dieting, marriage, grandmothering, death, Jonestown, world hunger, the nuclear threat, capital punishment, and the ERA are only a few of her subjects. Overriding them all is the theme of hope (to which) Layton came the hard way, through a difficult childhood, five children, a "shameful" divorce, bouts of manic-depression, mental hospitals, electroshock, contemplated suicide and the death of a son, after which, at her sister's suggestion, she signed up for a drawing course at nearby Ottawa University.

Since being discovered by Don Lambert, a young reporter for the *Ottawa Herald*, Layton has been crowned with honors. "Elizabeth Layton had gone through the whole course of modern psychiatry and it hadn't really changed her life. Then she takes up drawing and cures herself," marvels artist/therapist Robert Ault (1986, p. 149).

"Just to be myself," no matter what the world says, no matter one's inner critical voices, to find one's own way to live comfortably and congruently, to heal ourselves as Elizabeth Layton did, not "maybe" but *surely* "that's enough."

Chapter 10

Internalized Ageism

An attack of ageism began on me in the night and, sadly, continues this morning. It might have something to do with the fact that I am going to a neighbor's funeral later today but I don't think so. I hardly knew the woman who died only a few hours after a stroke. Sixty-nine is not old enough to die. What is old enough? Certainly not 59, my age. I choose 95 as the age at which I think I will die, based on genes, lifestyle, and zest for life. The truth is that my choice is based on longing and on wanting every minute I have coming.

In the midst of another time of change in my life, I am trying to reduce the number of things I do and speak more honestly to my friends, and to my husband of 37 years. When I overschedule and overcommit, I become tense and high-strung, and complain about how much I have to get done. However, now that I try to do less each day, my anxiety still rises.

What if there is nothing underneath all my activity and commitments, no meaning in my work, in leading values classes and women and aging groups, in writing, and in the support of alternative organizations and social justice causes? If I had no work, or did nothing I thought was of value, would my life still be worthwhile?

Last night and this morning, my life feels like a stupidly concocted sham, one that has fooled only me. There is not enough time left for what I want to do, and none of it matters anyway.

I am becoming old and am furious at my invisibility to men, at being patronized by younger people. Since I have lived in the same community for a long time and am very active, I do not experience the true invisibility of the aging woman. Perhaps it is sexual invisibility I am angry about, and the feeling that I am undesirable.

Nothing helps in the midst of this attack. Last night, with two hours home alone and no job immediately pressing, I checked the TV schedule and was entranced to watch a film on animals of the Serengeti Plain in Tanzania, Africa. At its end, I could only ask in self-pity: Have I found a place on this globe that calls me home, as did the narrator of the documentary?

Later, on a friend's recommendation, I watched Masterpiece Theatre. The acting was awful, the story thin and uneven, even banal — a troubled teen-age boy hung out with two girls one summer, had sex with them both; and his mother ended an unhappy affair with an arrogant, upper-class man. Again I was beset with anger and regret. Why had I not had sex as a young, single woman? What stupid need to be a "good girl" kept me feeling guilty about sexual behavior? Am I sexually desirable in my old age?

My husband found a joke in a magazine, that he added to his repertoire, about two women in a nursing home who decided to streak their fellow residents. Two startled old men looked up and one asked, "What was that?" "I don't know," the other replied, "but whatever they were wearing sure needs ironing." My husband did not understand how hurt I was by that joke, by that ridicule of women's aging skin and by the double standard that does not make a mockery of men's aging skin. He insisted it was my feminism, not any ageism in him that kept me from knowing the joke was harmless.

Am I an object of scorn as my body ages? Or do I only lack a sense of humor? When I related this incident in a speech on aging, a woman in the back raised her hand and asked: "Yes, but haven't you heard the one about the man who flashed the flower show at his nursing home and won first prize for best dried arrangement?" The room exploded in laughter. My husband did not think her joke was so funny. But I began to wonder if a sense of humor might not help me through these difficult times.

In the night, my mind and inner criticizer got together and found every little thing they could with which to beat me. The attack was quite overdone, since even I could tell, at three in the morning, how ludicrous it was. Thus this morning I am tired and have an emotional hangover that frightens me.

What am I doing in the middle of the stream of aging? How can I change this old self-critical behavior that I can no longer afford? How can I avoid self-rejection because I am an old woman being leveled by these self-inflicted attacks?

The attack passed by early afternoon. I went to the funeral, at a church I used to belong to and where our children went to Sunday School. (See Chapter 13: Reflections on a Funeral.) After a miserable hour, I fled from the church and over lunch talked to a friend who listened with love and understanding, and helped me get in touch with my own inner wisdom.

My inner self may have been trying to tell me not to do "the proper thing," not to go to the funeral as an act of neighborhood solidarity, which is what I told myself I was doing. I may have been warning myself not to go back to a place that espouses something I no longer find truth or life in, not to go back to that place in which I once looked for solace and reality, and where I had found neither.

For some reason, I was vulnerable and unable to avoid the attack of the "self-hater," as Starhawk (1982, pp. 37, 63), a writer and feminist spirituality leader, calls it. My strong reaction to the Christian funeral made me stop self-hating. It became an experience of knowing where I do not belong, of recognizing that I have changed a lot, and affirming that I need to trust and listen more carefully to what my deeper insides tell me.

The point, I think, of meditation, of writing in one's journal, of having friends to whom we can tell everything, is to carry us through these sloughs of despair. I can learn not to listen to the vultures that say my life is not authentic, and find, instead, under all the clutter and convention, that true self that loves and creates life, no matter what the circumstances.

Chapter 11

The Grief of Aging

"What about the grief of aging?" my friend Betty asked. Knowing about my work and preparing a church class on aging, she asked a question I had tried to avoid. There is grief in aging, I told her, and immediately wondered inside myself how to overcome that — rushing into solution even before acknowledging the problem, feeling the grief.

What do we grieve, and for how long? I asked myself. A woman in a 12-step group (recovery from addictions based on the 12 steps of Alcoholics Anonymous) told us that she had gone to see her favorite movie for the second time over the weekend and it made her feel terrible. The ghastly "Pretty Woman" was her current favorite and she now felt sad and depressed that she was no longer young, no longer viewed as sexy in the eyes of the world, no longer, I suppose, able to be courted and chased by a man who wanted to possess her. "And yet," she added, "my life was not so wonderful then either but I still want that." What a perfect, hideously painful, stuck place for aging women!

This woman, in her early 50's, was reed-slim, small, beautifully-dressed, attractive, employed and her gray hair done in fashion. She spoke, on another occasion, of not being able to fulfill her plans, two of which were to get in touch with her feelings and to lose weight. I winced to hear these contradictory aims — that she must fight her small body and lose weight in order to stay attractive and yet also want to let herself feel and express her feelings.

What happens to us when we age and hear things such as one woman heard from a friend back from her 30th high school reunion? "I felt so sorry for the fat women," the friend reported. "Their faces are still so pretty."

What about the grief felt by a stunning woman who had become a therapist in her late 40's, lamenting that she felt the loss of her maiden years to the disease of alcoholism? She must now "not choose mutilation" when offered the choice between a surgeon's knives and a crone's wrinkles.

Where is my own grief? Is it taken out in anger at institutions and people, at my own aging body, or is it projected on my husband, as he projects his culturally-enforced vision upon me, who is no longer young nor thin? In anger at his comment on "nice figures" or "she still looks good" remarks? Watching television one night, I pointed out to my husband a former colleague of his, the same age, on the screen. "My god, he's an old man!" my husband exclaimed, his face reddening as he realized he was describing himself. I easily see his aging denial and bewilderment, but not so easily my own. I find my own denial manifested in my anger at my husband's projections.

How do we face, acknowledge and work through our own grief at the loss of youth? We are most apt to hear, either from others or from our internal voices, that such grief is hardly to be valued, that there are so many grievous things wrong with the world today that to grieve old age — when we should be grateful to be alive — is middle-class luxury and narcissism in the extreme. How often do we talk about aging and someone always reminds us, cleverly, pointedly and judgmentally, of "the alternative."

"What about the grief of aging?" Betty asked. I do not know the answer. I suspect it must be plowed through so that it is not a constant, nagging issue, forever clouding and stalling our energies for getting on with our lives. To recognize that it is real and powerful might be the first step, to acknowledge that there is loss associated with aging, especially for women, and that we must grieve that loss in whatever way we can, frees us to accept and celebrate our aging.

A brilliant and seminal article on "Ageism and the Politics of Beauty" by Cynthia Rich (1990, pp. 6-10) is the most complete and succinct analysis of this subject I have read. Rich asks:

> How can we begin to change? We can — especially those of us in our forties and fifties — stop the trend of examining in public how disgusted we are at the thought of the bodily changes of growing old. . . . We can recognize that ideas of beauty are socialized into us and that yes, Virginia, we CAN begin to move in the direction of re-socializing ourselves. We can work

(for ourselves and for any revolution we might imagine) to develop a deeper and more resonant — dare I say more MATURE — concept of beauty.

Rich concludes:

I am looking at two photographs. One is of Septima Clark, on the back of the book she wrote in her late eighties about her early and ongoing work in the civil rights movement. The other is a postcard of Georgia O'Keeffe from a photo twenty years before her death. The hairs on their scalps are no longer a mass, but stand out singly. O'Keeffe's nose is "too" strong. Clark's is "too" broad. O'Keeffe's skin is "wizened," Clark's is "too" dark. Our task is to learn, not to look insultingly beyond these features to a soul we can celebrate, but instead take in these bodies as part of these souls — exciting, individual, beautiful.

Chapter 12

Becoming Old

I have spent the decade of the 1980s becoming old, not that I count my life in decades. In my late forties I was insouciant about being thrown into an aging crisis, so described by my therapist at that time. Then I was still thin, my dyed hair looked natural and felt comfortable to me, and I had not yet experienced any of what are called the ravages of old age.

Neither have I felt any such ravages now. I am healthy, active, limited only by energy, money and conditioning from doing as I wish. I have not been required to change my living arrangements, am completely able to take care of myself and my house, drive my car, travel and carry my own things.

As I approached age 50, at some level in my being, I began to face the prospect of no longer being young, but knew none of the physical or psychological facts of aging. Now I know some. I no longer feel attractive. To whom, I ask myself? To men, while in the company of other women and around my beautiful young daughters. The false standard of attractiveness to which I gave unconscious allegiance for years is a hard habit to break. In our culture, women are attractive when they are sexually useful and/or caregivers. An occasional Mother Teresa is admired for her wisdom but that is a tiny category. Old women are seen as sexually useless, gray hair and heavier than size 10 not among the attributes of sexually attractive women.

Singer Ronnie Gilbert (Mitchell 1990, p. 35), says:

> Older women are often relegated to "wise woman" status. We're not perceived as having love lives or problems of our own. It's as if a person's life as such gets wiped out by younger people who cannot imagine it. But we are sexual, we are

working, we have questions about what our lives are about.
. . . My partner . . . is nineteen years younger than I am, and
most of my friends are her age. I really have to try hard to
connect up with older women. . . . But how can younger
women make space? Everyone, including me, has been taught
to devalue age. Who wants to hear the old stories? Who has
the patience to hear them? We've lived longer — we have more
to relate. . . . When I had my fiftieth birthday, it was like
liberation day. I had this huge phony responsibility lifted off
my shoulders — a phony responsibility to be a certain way, to
be young . . . all the phony ideals about sexual stuff that have
nothing to do with the real sexual stuff. . . . It's a cheat that we
fear age so much.

I consciously chose to let my dyed hair grow out, to become one
with my aging sisters, and to stop passing for one of the "unusually
attractive" older women. After years of thinking I was overweight,
and most of that time fitting perfectly into size 10 clothes, I slowly
gained about 20 pounds, and went through a well-known diet program, successfully. The weight I lost and more "came" back on.
Two years after that weight gain I am finally searching for clothes
that are not too tight and that feel good on me, no matter what their
size. Old illusions die slowly, and sometimes agonizingly.

At best, I am having an interesting time learning to live by ideas
I'd only mouthed before, i.e., beauty is in the eye of the beholder;
attractiveness is not determined by body size, hair color and
makeup; old is beautiful; and aging is glorious, not ugly, bad nor
wrong. I had kidded myself for years that I believed lots of glorious
things about inner beauty. It is like being put through an Outward
Bound course in aging, that difficult experience of refining and re-
defining some of one's old truths.

I am embarrassed to discover that I have put so much stock in
appearance and that my confidence is lowered when I can no longer
depend on the surface definition of attractiveness. A more mature
and socially conscious person might ask, "Who cares?" Almost
anything in this world is more important. Yet I must acknowledge
that, for me, becoming an old woman poses some internal losses,
even if they are superficial. Both on conscious and unconscious

levels, I am a faithful follower of my culture, or at least have been until recently. That culture tells me not to age, to disguise both my aging and my feelings about it, and that to become old is awful and embarrassing. In order not to show aging or to be discounted as old and useless, and of course to keep women's power tied to patriarchal service, women must appear active, thin, and apparently financially well-off. At least it appears to me that I must be so in order to keep my worn-out place in the attractive woman category.

Men get to age and be distinguished in that process. Not so for women. The old women I saw recently and criticized, who were playing bridge at a Holiday Inn, rail-thin, hair-dyed, high-heeled, heavily made-up, clothed in Ultrasuede, were simply following the rules their culture communicated to them via the media, fashion and internalized ageism spouted by men and sometimes ourselves.

Not being caught in that double bind leaves its own bind. I could go back on a diet, and stay on one forever, fighting my body. I could dress more fashionably, wear makeup more often and put it on with more care, and figure out a more attractive fashion for gray hair other than slightly short, straight, and blown-dry at my swimming pool. That effort now goes into things I value more in my life. Maybe I am fooling myself, not wanting to make the effort to look like who the culture says is attractive.

If I do not follow what my culture says, what do I follow? What *are* valid guidelines and how do I recognize them? My answer is to listen to one's body, one's intuition, one's inner guidance and to check that out with a trusted friend; to read things that validate us as old women and teach us anew to honor ourselves; to ask questions and "question authority," as my favorite bumper sticker exhorts; to get together with other women who are making the same journey and seek out role models of healthy aging. We need community and affirmation for this time of rediscovering and recreating ourselves.

Talking with a friend a few years ago about who I really am, I wailed in not-such-mock indignation, "Well, I can hardly go around town looking like Emma Goldman!" "Why not?" she wanted to know.

Aging is no longer academic. I live right in the midst of many of its ambiguities, its sadnesses, its joys and compensations, and its profound and disturbing changes.

Chapter 13

Reflections on a Funeral

The minute I sat down in the crowded church, I wanted to run. Glancing across the aisle, I looked for an unobtrusive exit. I decided to concentrate on staying through the funeral service and on ways to affirm myself in the midst of the unexpected emotional explosion I was experiencing.

The funeral was for a neighbor, someone we waved at, called hello to, and who, with her husband, we saw occasionally at social functions; a salt of the earth couple. Even though I do not go to funerals unless it is for someone I knew well, some social propriety made me go to represent my husband and myself.

I was angry before I got to the church, angry, for one thing, that the honorary pallbearers were all men. With no heavy lifting to do, I thought, why, in god's name, could the honorary pallbearers not have been her women friends?

We sat in rows surveying the back of each other's heads, hearing scripture after scripture (of course Proverbs 31 was included: "A good wife . . . is far more precious than jewels. The heart of her husband trusts in her and he will have no lack of gain. She does him good. . . .") mostly emphasizing that Jesus Christ had risen from the dead, and that we, too, do not die.

We heard of the good wife who stands behind her family, nurtures them, cares for them, and is applauded for not caring for herself. We heard from the patriarchal church — represented by men in black dresses ranging themselves in pulpits above our heads — that there is no death in Christ, that we can, by force of will, act of mind or belief, rise above being dead. We heard about Jesus far more than the woman whose funeral it was and always heard God referred to as "He."

I was so angry I could hardly sit still. What let me forget and come to a place that preached things I no longer found substance in? What made me think I could do this for appearance's sake and get away with it? Singing old hymns comforted me and yet the words also sounded ridiculous. Figuring that any odd behavior of mine would be construed as grief, I wiggled, held my head in my hands and fidgeted with the program. These are good people, I told myself. Lots of them work at the Gathering Place Soup Kitchen. I struggled not to make them the enemy in order to find diversion for my anger.

Why do we know some people, I wondered, only when they die? Are we so busy, so afraid of intimacy that we trade in surfaces? I knew nothing of this woman's real self, much less the biographical data listed in the newspaper. When my sister Jane died last fall after a three-year battle against cancer and its cures, I was sad to discover how little I knew of her; her likes and dislikes, her friends, and that she was much more than the limiting phrases and memories of our family myths.

As we grieved, we knew any one of us could be dead at any moment. The woman had a stroke Sunday afternoon and was dead before her family got her to a hospital. It is good that she died instead of living on in a coma, yet the suddenness of her death brought her mourners face-to-face with their own mortality.

My anger was compounded by grief and sadness, and that what once worked for me no longer does. I spent a good part of my adult life searching for truth in a system in which it was only possible for me to find conformity in its rigid, narrow, concretized structures.

I thought up a new system to protect myself from such experiences: No more rituals in Christian churches, even though friends will die and I will want to attend their services. How long will I go on attending public rituals to prove I am a dues-paying, proper-behaving member of this society?

In junior high, my oldest daughter, Annie, strongly resisted taking a confirmation class at this same church, where I wandered the halls and sat Sunday after Sunday desperate for the comfort, love, acceptance and understanding that I could not find inside myself. In order to get Annie to go, she and I made a deal: if she took the confirmation class, she was free to choose to join the church or not.

She put up with what she and her friend Becky considered meaning-less, indefensible teachings from a minister and never looked back at the institution of the Christian church.

I observe that my three Sunday-schooled daughters are not angry at the church. They know full well that the church offers them noth-ing and pay it no attention. They appreciate the church (as I do) for its work in Third World countries, sheltering refugees, offering its basements as meeting places to thousands of Alcoholics Anony-mous groups, running shelters and soup kitchens, and offering ways to do social justice to their members.

I was once chagrined and embarrassed at my daughter's decision not to join the church. I never made choices and decisions with that kind of confidence and insouciance when I was her age. I am no longer an adolescent and am moving toward that kind of healthy, instinctive and intuitive wisdom shown years ago by my daughters, who were willing to risk being themselves. Beware wisdom! Be-ware old age!

The authentic journeys of becoming old do not make us nicer, nor more proper. Aging brings choices, changes and often discom-fort, as we live and move and have our being in our own hard-won, deeply-lived truth.

Chapter 14

Litany of a Death

PART I: NOT KNOWING
WINTER OF 1987-88

Often I write my way through difficult times. I did so when
my oldest sister was dying of cancer in 1988. Writing a story
and letting it form itself out of what I am experiencing keeps
me connected to my source, with my deepest, truest self. The
stories that follow are familiar; grief and bewilderment on the
occasion of a loved one's death. Especially as women age, we
need ways to come through the losses; no longer dependent on
organized religion, some of us are creating our own rituals to
bear the meaning of our lives.

All books, tapes, philosophies and strategies to the contrary, we
know so little about death. I do not know when my sister will die or
whether she will die from the cancer in the right half of her chest
and back, and lymph system, or from the damage inflicted on her
body by radiation and various chemotherapies.

Neither do I know how I feel about her dying except to remind
myself that we are all terminal. I know my unexpressed feelings
about Jane's dying reflect how I feel about my own death.

I feel heavy and tired, am preoccupied and occasionally dis-
traught. I am powerless in the face of Jane's injured, frightened
self, unable to bring into my consciousness any appropriate thought
or wisdom about death and the parting we are going through.

There is terrible ambivalence in our family, in every family I
suppose, about death. We do not know how long Jane will live nor
what she experiences as she goes through these days, exhausted,

unable to do anything but take pills and wander through her house and nap.

We do not know what we would have done differently, were Jane not dying. We think we know, but her dying makes what we could have done or been to one another, unhappily and slowly irrelevant.

We cannot fix any neat truth upon her life, nor come up with some noble truth illuminated by her dying and eventual death. Two of her three sons cannot face their mother's dying and, for the most part, stay away; her husband of 39 years stays home from his business and tenderly cares for her each day.

I do not say the wonderful things to Jane that I plan to each time before I come to visit. Who am I to give her permission to leave us, when I have paid little attention to my oldest sister during the 40 years of my adult life? We talk about her struggle against the cancer, her battle against this irrational disease. We do not talk about what it is like to know that you are dying. Jane's big gray eyes in her white face tell of her fear, her uncertainty, her tiredness, her despair and confusion. I have trouble knowing who is the dying Jane and who is the person she has always been.

Over and over again, I tell myself that death is part of life's natural cycle, that we all die, that I can grieve the loss of my sister while still accepting its inevitability. No one escapes, I remind myself, nor do any of us live without the circumstances of friends, family and ourselves being ill, dying, and troubled.

I who read as naturally and essentially as breathing, cannot stand more than a few pages of the books that others say have helped them through a death. Knowledge will not get me through this one.

When we talk, Jane apologizes for having tunnel vision; able to concentrate only on her condition, on getting some soft food or liquid down her damaged throat, fighting the nausea, taking all the pills at the right times, marshaling her half-paralyzed vocal cords for one more telephone visit or a few words to visiting family and friends, finding a bearable position for her swollen and nearly useless right arm, someplace to hold her tiredness, or some circumstance that puts her fear and bewilderment at bay.

Alive and healthy, I concentrate on my life, my tunnel vision is that of trivia, details and things to get done every day. It is a wonder that we can communicate with one another at all, all of us, burdened, confused and obsessed as we are with the minutia of ourselves.

I went to see Jane for a weekend, for what we both thought was to be the last time. It was not. I was desperately glad for the presence of our other sister Ann that weekend, which rescued me from the depression that settled within an hour after I got to Jane's house.

Jane, Ann and I went through Jane's considerable collection of jewelry, laughing and remembering, playing dress-up one last time. Ann and I fixed meals and talked quietly when Jane was napping, and encouraged her to take a few bites of food. Whenever Jane said something, I responded quickly, not in that desultory manner we often use with people who are not dying, by getting close to her and facing her as if she were deaf, trying to help her preserve what little was left of her ability to make sounds.

Ann and I took walks and we watched some basketball playoff games together with Jane's husband. I gave Jane a couple of backrubs and we all shifted our sleeping/waking clocks to Jane's early bedtime. We called our mother and reported our activities to her and were the visiting aunts to Jane's children. We tried to coax words from a mostly silent Jane, constantly asking her how she was doing.That is all we did, nothing dramatic. There is nothing dramatic about not knowing.

A cab driver, who brought me home from the airport, told me she drives a cab in the afternoon and counsels terminally ill patients in the mornings. Telling her of my visit, I said lamely, "I don't know." "That's the hardest part," she responded, "that we don't know." I was ready to get out of the cab the minute it stopped to avoid any sympathy or unwanted comments from her. She said only, "You have some thinking to do this afternoon." That is right. I have some thinking to do, some paying attention to my life and some not knowing to live with.

PART II: ANGER
EARLY SPRING 1988

We do the craziest stuff when someone is dying — act scared, talk in hushed tones, speak in euphemisms, deny it in subtle and sophisticated ways, and fight with each other.

Anger shoots out of me as from a child's water pistol yet not with any accuracy. I have almost given up trying to rationalize that certain situations and people justify my anger these days. I am angry that my sister Jane is dying and that I can do nothing about it. I get angry at myself for such powerlessness. Most of the time I deny my anger and focus on others and their current malfeasances.

I am also preoccupied. I tell myself to put a chicken in the oven to cook for supper and find, at suppertime, that I forgot to do it. My mind is so jumbled I cannot remember to tell anyone anything.

Sister Jane, whose body is exhausted from two-and-a-half years of cancer and its "remedies," is getting what she needs by dying; things such as attention, love, affection, touching, telephone calls and visits from her sisters. She has never had so much attention and love before. I think that knowledge must be bitter in her heart.

It has just dawned on me that sister Ann is the family caretaker. When our mother had a stroke last week, it was Ann who took charge, arranging for mother's stroke-disabled husband to go to a nursing home and taking charge of mother's affairs. It was Ann, 35 years ago, who was with mother when our father was taken to a Veterans' Hospital 100 miles away, never to return; the family home was sold and mother moved to an apartment. I am glad that I at last know about Ann and deeply appreciate and respect her role in the family. Surely now I can stop competing with her for mother's attention and approval.

A death that is consciously experienced has a lot to tell us. I am learning that underneath Jane's obnoxious, maddening, gauche exterior lies a tender, sensitive heart, one hurt long ago and not able to live without her fortress-like ego's protection. I recognize the bond between my mother and sister Ann; the middle child perhaps finding her worth by being the family caretaker.

In the face of death I see mother unable to manage, control or even understand. What is to be understood about a middle-aged daughter dying before her 82-year-old mother? I see mother's grief and lots of feelings she has kept bottled up for many years.

I keep my feelings buried, too, as if their expression would leave me out of control, unable to ever put myself back together again. I recognize my sideways anger, my denied grief. I criticize myself for agonizing over death, for being unable to accept with any grace or understanding this natural part of life, as if we were the only family ever to face such pain and confusion.

My middle daughter Mary tells me to remember that I am not running the show, that my job is to pay attention to my life, even as I telephone my mother daily and go one more time to my sister's house.

Death has much to teach me. In all this denial and grief and powerlessness, at least I know I must experience this and am not able to read my way through nor find any solace in thinking.

Teachers appear when we are ready, the saying goes. One of my teachers is the late Loren Eiseley, a Nebraska-born paleontologist and writer of exquisite prose. He spoke of the hidden teacher, for him a dream, a spider, nature. Some of our hidden teachers never show their faces and remain unconscious, coloring our lives without our knowledge or understanding. Even though I feel I am not ready for whatever teacher Jane's death and dying is, reality would indicate otherwise.

PART III: ANXIETY
LATE SPRING 1988

These are the days of my anxiety. I do not know which circumstance in my life is responsible for it. I remind myself to breathe deeply, knowing only that my emotional condition is like that of water roiling deep beneath the ocean's surface.

We all face death, separation and change. We keep on with our ordinary lives, go to work, fix food, talk to others, show up, answer the telephone, do the wash, get dressed, read the papers, and let the cat in and out. Maybe the ordinary saves us during difficult times. I read once about Kampuchean refugees crammed into camps, the men standing around with nothing to do, the women mending the fishing nets as they had always done. By having their ordinary job to do, the women were less vulnerable to despair, holding their lives together with the mending.

The saving grace of these days of my life, which are too full of grief and powerlessness, is having things to do. If I were left to live only in this state of anxiety, I think I would fly apart. When I feel like I am flying apart, I remember that there is a class to teach, a letter to write or soup to make. These tasks are not "stuffing" my feelings but keeping me from being overcome by fear, one of which is for my mother recovering from a stroke.

I make time for another weekend trip to my sister's house where she lies bald, scared and sick, sleeping a lot, the cancer in her body no longer, if it ever was, amenable to radiation and chemotherapy. Even though I doubt my ability to sit by her side with any serenity, I do not doubt my need to be with her one more time.

There are other causes of this late spring anxiety, such as the apparent failure of an organization I helped found, and a five-week trip to Peru full of nameless fears for me. Yet I wonder if anxiety does not lie just beneath the surface, waiting to snatch at something to feed its insatiable appetite. When I awake frightened, filled with terror, there is a second in which I know that death has come to visit, external circumstances only its messengers.

I dare not let my anger be triggered by the trivial. Friends and lovers are more precious, and are not to be injured or driven away by my outbursts of pain. Passion for such passing interests as the political primaries and other more local exasperations are off limits to me now.

I cling to some semblance of a schedule, even though I know there is not enough time for what must be done; there is never enough time, as we count it. Christmas comes, ready or not; the airplane takes off on schedule, and not when I am ready and have remembered to pack everything. Sickness, death, change and separation cut short what we intend to do.

I think I am not a victim of forces beyond my control, even though I understand our ultimate powerlessness. I choose to go be with my sister one more time. I feel sad to think of my indomitable 82-year-old mother, small and frail in her hospital bed. I want to keep my marriage alive, despite our wildly differing world views, our separate schedules, current and past misunderstandings and the tension of this time.

A long time ago I read that anxiety and depression are our bodies' attempts to tell us something, each an appropriate response to some inner or outer condition. Depression, an expert said, is a need to shut down and protect one's self, while anxiety is something that wants to be heard, but is usually ignored.

This spring engraves itself on my heart, a time when life interfered with my illusions, a time when the only safe passage between anxiety and depression is in the plain, ordinary, daily keeping-on. This place is how I get strength, courage and connection enough to survive this troubled sea of my life.

PART IV: JANE
AUTUMN, 1988

I do not remember much about my sister Jane's life. She is sleeping most of the time now, at home, and is frightened when she is awake. The breast and lymph node cancer in her body cannot be halted by massive doses of chemotherapy, her right side is burned by radiation, half her vocal cords are paralyzed, her right arm is swollen and useless, immobilized by fluid retention, and her body rejects solid food. She can only sleep sitting up in a chair or propped up in bed.

My other image of Jane is that of a tall, dark-haired, slim young woman. Jane was beautiful. Difficult years and life itself took away that 22-inch waist, the long brunette hair, even the easy smile.

Jane had a horse when we were growing up, a roan gelding named King. She could handle him. My sister Ann and I hated King, and were scared of his rearing and bad temper. I think we projected onto Jane's horse one of our family myths about Jane, and perhaps she did, too, in order to have an ally. We always said that Jane had a terrible temper. She also brought home socially unacceptable friends, was rather awkward, and did not fit our definition of how one was to act.

For some reason of her own, Jane did not aspire to be a cheerleader or a scholar, perfectly natural goals for Ann and myself. How, then, could she be defined, especially by my parents or her more extroverted and apparently socially adept sisters? Jane played the piano well; Ann and I cheated on our hour-a-day practice requirement. Jane rode King expertly and hung around with her different friends. She did attract her share of worthy boyfriends, a redeeming quality.

Jane says what all first children say: that mother and dad learned how to parent on her. She remembers not being allowed many privileges, and insists that Ann and I were permitted many things denied to her. She fought with our tyrannical father and earned, instead of freedom, the label of terrible temper in our family's dispensation of titles.

She graduated from high school in 1945, attended a local college for one year and then went to the state university where she pledged a good sorority. But true to form, Jane was not interested in our mother's sorority, offending them with her error of not wanting to be a member of what was considered the best group. After her sophomore year, Jane married at 19. She had four babies within five years and lived in dusty Wyoming towns — maintaining the fiction that she was a member of some elite, while she really suffered years of financial struggle.

To my family's dismay, Jane weighed a lot in her adult years and occasionally spent money in what was considered to be unwise ways. Only in the last ten years of her life has she had some fun; bowling, playing bridge and pinochle, socializing with the spouses of her husband's Rotary Club members, and at her husband's business conventions.

She has always watched soap operas a lot, taping conflicting shows on another TV set. Although an enormously proud person, Jane has not a vain bone in her body when it comes to enjoying what I consider banal and tacky.

A few years ago I began to see a wise and tender heart under Jane's rough extrior, and I am grateful for that new vision. It is still difficult for me, though, to give up my armor of superiority in order to fully appreciate my sister. As she dies, I am caught between that old regretful attitude and this new one, feeling I am too late and undoubtedly powerless to set things right.

No one in our family ever saw things from Jane's perspective, certainly not me. All these 60 years she has seen us better perhaps than we have known ourselves, by virtue of being the outcast, the one who did not fit into our ideal of who she was supposed to be. At death, we realize we did not know or love the person well enough. I grew up with my sister Jane and never felt the deep connection of sister until now, as she dies.

PART V: DEATH
DECEMBER 1988

My oldest sister died this November after a three-year struggle against cancer. Now I know some things I did not know before, deep in my gut, not just in my head. Dead is very different from dying. Dead is final, cannot change and is no longer dying. For a long time I have thought of Jane each day and prayed for her as she went through the various stages of dying. Now, each day, I remember that she is no longer dying. She is dead.

Surely an unexpected death is harder to accept than one you know is coming. People say you grieve ahead of time for the person who is obviously dying. I am not sure; I think any death is a shock and changes things in a way that dying does not. The death of someone you are connected to changes your world. Jane's death changed mine. Something is forever different, for her family and friends, for my mother and my sister Ann and me. I am reminded of a family systems mobile, where change in one part affects all the other parts.

People born of the same mother are connected in a way beyond their doing. Jane and I were not close and were connected only in conventional ways. Yet she is still my sister. When she died, I felt (and still feel, more than a year later) as if Ann and I were only two-thirds of a whole.

When we gathered in Spokane in the days before and after Jane's memorial service, Ann and I looked at each other in dismay and grief. She and mother and I clung to each other after the funeral, as if we were all who were left.

Grief makes people act oddly. A collection of people grieving, trying to interact normally, is a dismaying and yet occasionally heartening thing. There is a huge tendency not to talk about the dead person, and in fact to talk of things totally or wildly irrelevant. I reacted oppositely, trying to talk about Jane and to get everyone else to, as well.

I discovered that I know very little about my sister. The family myth of her is hardly complete. I am sad for the part I played in maintaining that myth. I did not know and chose to ignore much that was good about her: that she read a lot of decent books, did lovely handiwork, had many good friends, and could not do enough for those she knew and loved.

A lot of old stuff gets brought up by a death in the family, especially the unhealed, ignored things, like jealousy, blaming, abandonment and rejection. It is as if old behaviors and attitudes became unwelcome guests in Jane's home, all of us trying to navigate around their heavy, unbidden forms in the rooms of her house.

I know nothing about life after death. Yet I wonder if Jane's spirit is still around, feeling unfinished, wanting something from us. Does she live on in us or is there some bodyless consciousness in which she exists? I barely accept from others the comfort of their saying or knowing that she is now at peace.

Cancer is an ugly disease, one whose "cures" wrecked my sister's body. The radiation paralyzed her vocal cords, damaged her esophagus and burned her chest and neck; the chemotherapy destroyed the blood-making mechanism in her bone marrow and, among other effects, made her scratch herself constantly, even to the point of scratching open her skin.

My brother-in-law tended Jane for three years, nearly always with love and tenderness. He cared for her and suffered silently through the times of her emotional pain, confusion and anger.

I thought my distance from Jane and the knowledge of her imminent death would make my last trip to Spokane, and these days after her death, easy for me. Self-righteously, I thought my wisdom would be helpful to myself and everyone else. Not so, not so at all. These days are very hard. Depression keeps me off-center. Its low-level presence in me has found a new source to make the Thanksgiving-Christmas-New Year's transit harder than usual.

I worry about how mother is handling this grief. Jane's dying was the hardest thing in her life; a life that had lots of hardships in it. Is Jane's death harder than her dying for that mother outliving her first child?

Everyone experiences death and tragedy. How in heaven, I wonder, do people go on with their lives without becoming bitter, self-centered or weighed down by their sorrow? How do we live in long-term partnerships and restructure our life when one dies? How do I face my own mortality? I do not want to spend the time left lamenting my inevitable death.

I know that time lessens grief, that this, too, shall pass. I put one foot in front of the other and do what needs doing. Exercise and meditation help. My sleep is disrupted and heavy, dreams working to bring order out of chaos. I feel alone and sickeningly insecure. Messages of comfort from friends reach into my psychic isolation. There are worse things than death and I know my sorrow is not unique nor to be borne too heavily nor laid on others.

I would not wish Jane to live on in pain and fear—nor to die. I am not in charge of that, if any *one* is. I need not find an explanation for her long dying. I wince at the revisionist history practiced by her children and husband. Yet my tiny part in knowing her probably sounds like fairy tales to them. We are finding a Jane we did not know, as her children go through her things and as we share our memories of her.

This season finds me, not strangely, unsettled and burdened, by the death of my sister Jane. I miss her more in death than I ever did in the miles and years and differences separating us while she lived.

> Part of the aging process must surely be both the knowledge and acceptance that for some things there are no answers, that some sadnesses are simply to be borne. I do not mean that we go galumphing through the years of old age, burdened with sorrow and pity, although some do. Even though I teach Values Clarification—which often asks "What is the next step?" and counsels action to incorporate our values into our daily lives—and though I know how much affirmative action aging women must take in order not to be swallowed up in an early death by the myth that we are useless and invisible, I recognize that not everything can be figured out, nor overcome. We especially need the healing presence of friends who hear and hold us and time that lessens our grief. Sometimes I agree with the rhetorical question of monk and mystic Thomas Merton, on an old Abbey Press card pinned to the bulletin board above my desk, "Does there always have to be a reason for everything?"

Chapter 15

Where Does the Time Go?

"Where does the time go?" Rhoda asked her friends one year on that good old TV program, *The Mary Tyler Moore Show*. "To Cincinnati," answered Ted. Every day, in each life, time goes and gets used up in a hundred things both planned and unexpected.

I constantly overestimate how much of my activity will fit into the hours and minutes in a day. Some time gets wasted; it keeps moving while I am standing still and/or doing nothing; its passage and my list do not fit; a lot of it gets used up in mundane details, most of which were not factored into my grand scheme of doing.

Aware of time or not, I get much done as I persist in planning and structure, thinking through the list of errands and chores; how much can be done before noon, after lunch, before supper, after supper, before bedtime. Poor day, carved into such unyielding sections!

"Where do the years go?" is what I am really asking these days. I cannot look back with any sense of completeness over the 59 years behind me. That is too long and with too much to remember except in chunks of experiences or little pieces of memory. My friend Keith Kinsolving has admonished me, though, to look back over my life and honor it, to reflect, she insisted, on all I've done and experienced. And my friend Fredrena, looking over some old resumes of mine, asked me if I wasn't terribly tired!

I have less than half of my life left to live. Knowing how finite a resource these years truly are, I am more conscious of how I am to use them. (Chapter 25 specifically addresses this.) Will I use what is left to me wisely, as I truly want to, or will life whiz by, seasons tumbling into one another, Christmasses, Easters, Fourths of July, semesters and tax deadlines piling up too fast, blurring into one another? I do not understand this psychological condition of aging, of time going faster the older one is, of years seeming like months. I thought I had a mammogram a few short months ago and, upon checking with my doctor, found it was more than a year ago.

"Where does the time go?" means, to me, under the joking, plaintive surface: "How can I make it matter, slow it down, make it reflective, full of meaning and purpose according to what I've figured out about Why I Am Here and What I Am To Do in this lifetime?" The meter runs no matter what. The length of this experience called life continues to roll out, wind up and wind down a fixed amount with the details differing only slightly at the end for those who make it into early old age.

Time goes by while working, sleeping, eating and shopping. It is consumed by reading, watching TV, talking, going from one place to another either fast or slow. Time goes by while studying and wondering and is used up in races and walks, in raising gardens and fixing meals. It is measured by the birth of children and the death of loved ones. It is counted in school years and number of years at a job. Some count it in money and property gathered. It is marked by seasons and days, sunrises, sunsets, vacations and holidays. We have new years, old times, and present moments.

Time swirls around in heads and shows on bodies. I act as if it were linear yet know in some corner of myself that it is spiral, circular, elliptical, without beginning or end. A day's worth of time registers more intensely than do past ages and, despite the work of a generation of futurists, it is hard to think about time beyond one's life or time available to one's descendants. Next week or next summer are closer, more real, possible and manageable.

The years of a life: how do they count? And to whom? Inside this time-counting person, I hope my years will span nearly a century; time is precious. Yet I waste it, think I have more of it than I actually do and that I will use it better than is probable. There is too little time left for me to hurry. I am not capable of saving a minute of time, nor of slowing its inexorable movement.

In an article in the May 26, 1990, *Lincoln Star,* (p. 10), "This Moment Most Valuable of All," I wrote of the sacrament of the present moment. "This hour, Sarah Orne Jewett said in a letter to Willa Cather, is worth more to you than anything you can do in it," I wrote. "What piece of what I call work is worth the loss of the

magic and mystery of this (Monday) morning?'' I asked, conclud-
ing that "this May morning has worth beyond my calculating, is
worth more than my industrious self can cram into its immeasurable
depths, this fragile, unheralded, time out of time.''

As I lament its passage, I remember that measuring time was
instituted to increase the work and prayer of monks. Bells chimed
on the quarter hour in 14th century monasteries, urging monks to
accomplish more. They ring more frantically as we age.

What does one do with the years? How that changes from youth
to middle to old age! Time comes and goes and is no more. As its
essence eludes me, time measures this life I live, one I understand
only slightly but which I love fiercely!

Chapter 16

A January Tale

This is a January tale, a time of winter blahs and post-holiday blues. It began in the laundry room as I reminded myself to change the furnace filter and immediately thought: "Oh, if I'd remembered to change the filter before the girls came home, they wouldn't have had such bad allergy attacks"—reasoning which ignored the presence of two furry cats.

The furnace filter moment was simply another in a long string of regrets that caught me after our grown-up daughters and my mother had gone back to their lives after Christmas. The regrets marched into my consciousness in an unbroken line of "Oh, I should have . . ." or "If I'd only . . ." or "Why didn't we . . .?"

The girls and I laugh ruefully at what we call terminal regret, so named since the day I recognized regret as a disease, not an unwritten rule of human existence to which we are obliged to pay attention. It is born of perfectionism run amuck, second-guessing, and adults clinging to the infant's perception that she controls the world.

Awareness is half the battle, one hears. If that is so, I am in good shape, since I am so painfully aware of all those things that didn't go "right" during the annual week we crowd into one house and do Christmas. It was too much and I got lost for a few days.

We had the most fun when we were taking walks together, or spontaneously grouped in the kitchen—eating, talking, laughing, answering the telephone, safe, warm, and contented.

The worst times for me—ever the mother/general—were handling the logistics of four people added to one house (such middle-class luxury!), sharing a car, reminding everyone of various appointments (chiropractic, massage and Feldenkrais, the home-spa package for all three daughters), getting a consensus on reservation times for meals out and what time which old family friends could stop over to see "the girls." And that is not all. The girls always plan to see their old friends, thrift-shop with one another, take naps, go to movies, and stay up late at night in the living room for real talking and their irreverent hilarity.

A leftover ham in the freezer and a smoked turkey in the fridge haunt me. "We should have had more meals in," the voice of worthless regret says. "We should have made more salads." "We should have had more unscheduled time." "Did I give everyone equal backrubs?" "How come I don't ask for backrubs, too?"

On and on it goes, a parasite on my soul, obviously prepared to live off me the rest of its life, which probably just matches my remaining time. A voice tells me that if I had just lived right, I could avoid regret's insidious self, dangling a carrot in front of my nose, held by a contraption attached to my own back collar.

Tennyson's "Oh last regret, regret can die" (from a line in the "Prologue" to *In Memoriam*) makes me think that only at death is regret done for. Does aging trigger regret more than it brings acceptance?

Henry James wrote to Hugh Walpole (August 21, 1913) that "I only regret, in my chilled age, certain occasions and possibilities I didn't embrace." Regret sounds real in those lines. Perhaps my naming it false is whistling in the dark. Taped to my desk are words by Alice James (Strouse 1980, p. 310), Henry's equally gifted sister: "It isn't in the sorrows and pains but in the inexorable inadequacy for happiness that the tragedy lies." Her words resound in my heart.

Perhaps regret is our way of choosing suffering, "to inhibit our self-reflection" as W. H. Auden (1975, p. 196) says in "For The Time Being." In that Christmas oratorio, Auden writes that we "stayed up so late, attempted — quite unsuccessfully to love all of our relatives, and in general grossly overestimated our powers." That we did. That we do.

This January I wash the sheets and remake the beds, gradually clean out the icebox and go to the hot tubs downtown, regretting, of course, that I didn't corral everyone home for Christmas into a hot tub session.

Surely the time is coming when I will simply refuse to regret anything—last year, stressful holidays, yesterday, how I am or was. I hope to be content with the bittersweet taste of work and love and my life, grateful, not regretful, of those wondrous things.

Chapter 17

Regret, Oh Damned Regret

In a cartoon by Cathy Guisewite, "Cathy" sits in her bathrobe and slippers at home, thinking:

> Things I should have done at work . . . Things I wish I'd said to Irving . . . Things I promised myself I'd never do again that I did anyway. Ways I made myself miserable that I could have avoided. Things I could have done for my family, my puppy, my friends, my co-workers, my neighbors, my finances, my home, my closets, my diet and millions of people in need whom I've never met.

She wryly concludes: "Even when I'm not going anywhere I have 300 pounds of luggage with me."

To lighten the emotional load of our aging years, we can take care of some of the unfinished business of our lives, whether that is to write a will, plant a garden, or make an amend. We are less burdened or obsessed by regrets as we talk and write about them; we can figure out if there is action we can take, or accept and let go. We need to find ways to release regret's power over us. We can laugh, cry and decide how much energy we want our regrets to take. To bring regrets into the light of consciousness keeps them from sniggering around our edges, keeping us ever mournful.

My favorite magazine, *The Sun*, invites its readers each month to write about a variety of subjects such as duty, kindred spirits, compromise, wealth, beauty, peak experiences, comforts, idols, visitors, and where I am now. The pages on Regret (1986) include treasures such as these:

Regrets drag you down unless they're being used in the present
to avoid the mistakes of the past.

I regret being in California when my grandmother died in
North Carolina. . . . But I do not regret the pain her death still
brings me.

Regret is a product of an erroneous relationship to time. . . .
Letting go of regret is largely, for me, a matter of learning to
flow with time, to get with it instead of against it. . . . As soon
as I accept the passage of time and the seasons, the disappear-
ances, the rebirths, I no longer feel alienated from it. I feel so
much a part of the process that a sense of loss becomes ridiculous.

In my novice days of therapy, I walked into my therapist's office
one day and announced that I was trying not to feel sorry for myself. She suggested that I feel self-pity before I tried to banish it.
Likewise I think we must face and feel our regrets before we can be
done with them.

In recent years I have been able to cut through my incessant second-guessing of myself by using Mamie Porter's Three Questions
(Simon 1978, pp. 74-80). Devised for teacher training, the questions are: (1) What do I like about what I did? (2) Next time, how
would I do it differently? (3) What help do I need from someone
else? A professor at Austin College, Texas, Porter insists that these
three questions are the *only* evaluation needed any time. These three
questions help me fight back against new regrets, the vultures that
wait to attack when I am tired, vulnerable, laboring under too much
to do, and even low blood sugar.

Writing for people whose partners have died, Widowed Persons
Service volunteer Hertha Olson reminds her readers in *Lifelines*, a
publication of The Lincoln (NE) Area Agency on Aging, "The 'if-
onlys' may win some battles but they can't win the war unless we
give up. Do something each day to give your day a backbone,
schedule your time, learn something new, treat yourself well."

I remember with joy these words written in a Women and Aging
class by Elizabeth K. Wilson, a courageous woman figuring out
how to support herself in her old age, with no retirement income,

living alone for the first time, and building a support network beyond that of her children:

> When considering regrets, one needs to sort them out: those
> that were small momentary lapses of courtesy or good judg-
> ment; those that were major decisions reached through careful
> evaluating, a specific set of circumstances or procrastination.
> As we sort, we need to distinguish between those things that
> are really painful regrets, those we could still change, and
> those that have an element of regret but some subsequent good
> results. . . . Regret will not alter what happened in the past. It
> is non-productive to continue to lament. Its one value is to
> avoid similar situations and forestall creating new regrets.
> Some regrets, appearing to be buried, still lurk beneath the
> surface. There might be some value in listing all your regrets
> and then see if you've forgiven yourself or another. If you
> haven't forgiven, do so, for regret is closely related to that
> most destructive force called guilt.

My own path through the bramble bushes of regret ranges from
the hardly-worth-noticing to major anguish. Self-criticism and self-
righteousness are behaviors I have to watch out for. My ego may
decide that something goes on the regret list that was never within
my power to affect at all. Things I thought I would regret forever
have lost their power over me. I know better now than to think that
the voice of regret must "never" or "always" be listened to. I
know my own regret to be a chimera, at times, an imaginary mon-
ster feeding on my deeply-held illusion that I am in control, of that
need to keep chaos at bay.

Many of our lives' twists and turns, its idiosyncrasies and idiocies, make us sad, make us want to live something over again, and
weigh us down with the burden of times imperfectly navigated.
There *is* sadness — the thing undone, the person unloved, the affair
had or not, the choice ignored, the moment not seized, the apology
not made. And yet we remember, as Annie Dillard (1989, p. 32)
says, "How we spend our days is, of course, how we spend our
lives."

At a poetry reading last week, this line jumped out at me: "The joy of leaving things unfinished. . . ." I could imagine how delicious that would be! I was equally comforted by reading in a review of Gertrud Nelson's *To Dance With God*, "She knows that less is more. Best of all perhaps, she appreciates profoundly how our aspirations and our longings must come to terms with our limitations and our failures."

Some discrimination is forming in me, in these aging years, in regard to regret—choices about, attending to, confronting, ignoring, letting go, finding the courage inside myself and with my sisters to become old, and less burdened with emotional baggage.

III. HONORING AND GATHERING OUR STRENGTH

Chapter 18

Interdependence: Support Groups

Next to the air we breathe, we are sustained by our friends. I think that friendships are second in importance only to oxygen — perhaps a slight exaggeration. We are tribal people and there is in the human condition a need to belong to the neighborhood, race, church, club, family, job or ethnic group. In truth, most people long for the deep satisfaction that comes from being known at the level of who they really are, that level that knows no boundaries. We profess and boast of a certain individualism, yet we constantly act out our visceral need for community in many and varied ways.

I have often thought that a wonderful place to grow old would be in the fellowship (I cannot find a gender-neutral word for fellowship) of Alcoholics Anonymous. Meeting several times a week with people you have something in common with — that you wrecked your life, your baby and brain, your emotional health, your family, and/or almost went crazy or died prematurely — forces basically lonely people to become socialized. The laughter and closeness one finds among AA members is good evidence that their meetings do more than keep them from using mind-altering chemicals, and that socialization may be a significant way to live without using such chemicals. AA cuts across lines of age, gender, nationality, race, religion, sexual preference, profession and both mental and physical ability.

AA provides a structure for support, company, help, wisdom, acceptance, a place that allows people to give up feelings of alienation and aloneness. Members "have to" go to meetings to sustain their sobriety. Most attend meetings in different places while traveling, and also connect with new groups in the process of moving.

In recent years, dissatisfaction has been expressed with AA's apparent insistence on referring to a "Higher Power." Several alternative organizations have been formed, two of which are: Secular Organizations for Sobriety, Box 5, Buffalo, NY 14215, founded by Jim Christopher; and Women for Sobriety, Inc., Box 618, Quakertown, PA, 18951, founded by Jean Kirkpatrick. I also recommend a powerful book by Jungian therapist Jan Bauer (1982) titled, *Alcoholism and Women: The Background and the Psychology*.

Women are sustained by women, especially as they age and in their old age. Women live longer than men; thus the need to make and deepen our relationships with one another now.

The bridge club is an unlabeled support group for many women. One may deride its social usefulness in this age when women work outside the home for economic survival or independence, yet these card-playing women have told their troubles and shared their joys over the years with one another. Twenty-five years of meeting weekly for a few hours, in a supportive friendly atmosphere, provides emotional health for many women.

Driving to Utah one summer, my husband and I chanced upon a meeting of the Bluebelles of Colby, Kansas, as we ate breakfast in a motel dining room. We watched these women pass around pictures of their grandchildren and great-grandchildren, read parts of letters, ask each other about their lives, and listen to each other. We found out later that these women had been meeting together for more than 50 years, growing old together. It was clear how much this group and its friendships meant to all of them — and, vicariously, to us, as we thought of our own need for friends who have known us a long time.

In Women and Aging groups, we make a chart of our friendships, showing the patterns of our support networks. We think of people we know in terms of family, friends and coworkers, and also which of our friends bring different support to our lives. We learn a lot about ourselves as we write down the names of our friends in categories: the friend we can tell everything to; the friend who brings us chicken soup when we are sick, literally or figuratively; the friend who encourages us to stretch intellectually; the friend who helps us monitor our health, suggesting an apple instead of a hot fudge sundae; sponsors and friends in 12-step groups; the friend who brings fun and adventure into our lives. A close friend calls herself the chairperson of fun, games and therapeutic outings. She is indeed that, and I love to be with her.

There are friends who are role models for us in areas such as aging, nutrition, vocation, fun, time alone, social justice work, honesty or spirituality. There are also friends whom I call my growing edge — persons who say things that upset me, who perhaps try too hard, who may want more of me than I can give, or even a holier-than-thou person — all mirrors of my unconscious self.

The women and aging groups find big gaps in our connectedness networks and realize that we too often depend on one person for most of our support. We see how limiting our ideas of friendship are. And we wonder what to do. We brainstorm ways to meet people with whom we have things in common (brainstorming rules: no put-downs, piggybacking encouraged, and anything goes. We often find wisdom in the absurd); ways to deepen a relationship with someone we care about; ways to clear out some of our busyness so that we have more time for healthy friendships.

Working on a friendship happily contradicts an unspoken rule I grew up with: that friendship just happens; you do not do anything so gauche as to make it happen or *work* on it. We *do* need to work on it. I might better describe the need to increase both the quantity and quality of our friendships by saying that we must give time and energy to someone we care about and who cares about us, without whose connection and nourishment we will shrivel up and feel bad about ourselves. Old age is a time to recognize how connected we all are in this world, this universe or in "that great household to which we all belong," in Reinhold Neibuhr's words, and to act that out in sustaining and nourishing friendships of all kinds, colors and sizes.

For people who want the support of an intentional group, I recommend the booklet *Support Groups: It Doesn't Have to Be You Alone Against the World,* by my friend and therapist Janet Twarogowski (1990).

A life nurtured and sustained by friendship, by that connectedness to the human family, is one that grows into old age with more courage and wisdom than one alone and a life with more awareness of how much strength women gain from each other. A poem titled "Courage" by Ellen Bass (1986), illustrated by Judy Claire Lieblein, sits, matted, on a wall in my office, reminding me of its simple, profound truth:

> In the grocery store I buy beets.
> My lover is coming to dinner tonight
> And she has asked for borscht.
> I choose the largest bunch: 89¢
>
> There is no sour cream.
> The aproned man tells me
> "Tomorrow morning." But my lover
> Is coming tonight.
>
> Leaving, I see headlines:
> "U.S. invades Grenada"
> Fear coils within my ribs
> And anger—that just as my life blooms
> Into sweetness, these idiots
> Up the ante.
>
> I feel foolish as I drive to another store.
> What does it matter
> If our borscht has sour cream or doesn't?
> But I buy the sour cream.
>
> I scrub beets, chop
> And put them to boil,
> Their rich red infusing the water.
>
> This too is courage:
> To cook, to eat
> To seize our daily lives.

Chapter 19

Heroines: Role Models

"If you meet the Buddha on the road, kill him," is good advice given by therapist Sheldon Kopp (1972) in his book of the same title. For some, the age of the guru is past, the time of listening to our intuitive, inner, archetypal wisdom now here. However, women need role models of people who embody the vision of who we are and who lend their presence to our journeys.

Dependence on another is a big issue for women struggling to come to consciousness. My friend Sister Adrian Hofstetter told me years ago that we have sat at the feet of men too long. Socialized to be passive and through learned helplessness, women have a harder time than men in wresting themselves away from unhealthy dependence on another or on a system, a guru in flesh or other form.

Women have too little experience in holding one another up as examples of courage, examples of anything, because for the most part, women's lives have been ignored in history.

In the last chapter, we explored connectedness networks, thinking of people who are role models, among the other friendship categories. Social scientists Harris Clemes and Reynold Bean (1983) identify four vital components of self-esteem, one of which is having role models who are doing it better than you are (more on their work in Chapter 23, Tools). Unfortunately that sounds like someone I've placed above me, someone I envy. Yet I find it healthy to admire and ask advice of women who are "doing it better" than I am. For instance, my daughter Mary is my nutrition role model and a superb one. She reads labels, shops mostly in health food stores, reads widely on nutrition research, rarely eats out, and pays attention to her body. I would not choose role models who are "doing it worse" than I am. Tennis players like to play with someone better than they are in order to improve their game.

I am grateful to have compañeras on my journey, people who walk with me, gentle faithful friends, even the therapist who fits the late Shelly Kopp's (1972) description: someone who walks with you until you regain your courage.

My innate tendency (probably socialized, not innate) is to put people on pedestals, especially women. I used to revere men and often secretly resented them for my allegiance. But women were elevated in my emotional landscape to authority figures, dispensing or withholding approval.

Having role models differs from putting people on pedestals. Adrian has long been my social justice role model, the person who gently encourages me to accompany her on many a journey, to speak out, to publicly witness to my values, to stand with people long involved in peace and justice issues.

My friend Kittu, twelve years older than I, is also a splendid role model of an older woman, plus an inspiration to me, through her healthy, wise, loving, vibrant self. The fact that she is all those things, and an aging woman who does not conceal her age under makeup, fashionable clothing, girlish behavior or coyness and does not despair in the face of old age, make her a strong role model. We share deep affection and respect for one another. Thus having Adrian and Kittu for role models is not one-sided. They are both naturally models of peer relationships, that of women empowering women.

Whether acknowledged or not, there are brave women role models — old women role models — all around us. Ask a woman and hear her fondly describe a neighbor, a grandmother, a mother, a nursing school teacher, a writer, an actress, an activist. Long before I became conscious of my own aging, I wrote a story entitled "If I can be Maggie Kuhn, then I'll go." I blush at the arrogance of thinking I had a choice in the matter of "going" but at least my instincts were on target. What I knew of Maggie Kuhn (1984) was that in her retirement years she founded The Gray Panthers, an advocacy organization for the old, and demonstrated courage, energy, grit, determination and intelligence. Besides admonishing us to "do something outrageous each day," she describes old age as "not a disease. It is strength and survivorship, triumph over all kinds of vicissitudes and disappointments, trials and illnesses" (Fields 1984, p. 95). How lucky we are to have a Maggie Kuhn leading the way into old age!

Eleanor Roosevelt, a wonderful role model, cannot love us back, yet one can still know her and gain strength from her as a brave woman who widened horizons for women, wives and women living in the glare of public life.

From Mother Teresa to the old woman across the street, we have each other to rely on, to learn from, to hold the vision of who we can be in our old age. (A friend overcommitted to the work of this world tells the story of standing in line behind Mother Teresa at Heaven's gate, hearing St. Peter ask the saint, "How come you didn't do more?")

Role models are examples of how to age, how to eat wisely, how best to utilize our energies in social justice, how to advocate for ourselves and other aging women — in health care, pension rights, housing benefits, tax laws, in countless areas, in knowing our boundaries and accepting our limitations, in assertiveness, in making of today that substance of which we want our tomorrow to consist. Such qualities that one envies or admires are latent in one's self. I am convinced that envy is a plumb line to our own capabilities and dreams. In describing old women we admire, we are describing our possible selves.

Women have always found each other; on the frontier of Wyoming, as in the film "Heartland," in the office, in feminism, at church, in the neighborhood, in old age and across the generations. We hold and empower the vision for one another, the vision of who we are now and are becoming, especially in old age.

Chapter 20

Being Response/able

My reach has always exceeded my grasp, never with more ferocity than in the years since I turned fifty. I do not know and probably shall never find that healthy balance between being and doing, that unmarked boundary between making things happen and letting them happen. However, in the meantime I keep lists. For groups of women reflecting on their aging, I designed a list called: How Response/able We Are — how able we are to respond to the circumstances of our lives.

Twelve areas in which we can assess our response/ableness are: finances/money, leisure time and social life, transportation, health, food, travel, living arrangements, organizations, legal matters, alone time, chores and relationships.

There are as many ways of approaching these life-areas as there are aging women, although some suggestions appeal more to some than to others. Some categories are more important than others and some overlap. These areas don't cover everything *nor are the following reflections exhaustive.* They are meant simply to suggest, to get women started being response/able where needed and to celebrate those areas where we already are.

Married or formerly married women respond quite differently to this exercise than do single women. Single women do not depend on a partner to take out the garbage or write a will.

In finances/money, one woman brought to her Women and Aging group an extension division pamphlet titled, "Property Statement and Family Objectives for Estate Planning." Another brought the Older Women's League's "Self-Sufficiency Assessment." Publications and seminars provided by community colleges, women's commissions and elder organizations are helpful to women who do not know how much income they will have to live on in old age. Help can also be found for those who need to face their finances with the appropriate information, in an atmosphere of planning and choosing, rather than staying prey to anxiety.

Leisure time and social life hardly seem like areas one needs to be intentional about. "Whatever time is left over" or "when someone calls" are traditional/typical attitudes toward leisure time and activities. Three healthy suggestions are: to use time in ways that please ourselves, to resist feeling victim to chores and jobs, and not to waste optional hours with television-staring, mall-wandering or worrying about others. Some women need to reach out to others, building a network of friends with whom to do things. "Things don't just happen. They require planning," says Dr. Jan Gault, a San Francisco-based leisure management specialist and author. "With planning, you can have a more creative, fulfilling life" (*Christian Science Monitor* 1985, July 15, p. 26).

Transportation and travel sound alike but are separate areas of our lives. Transportation, for example, means: Do you live near a bus line? How do you get the groceries home when you no longer drive? Are you in the habit of sharing rides? How will you manage such things when your body is less strong? Is transportation wheelchair-accessible in your area?

Travel asks us: Do you have enough money to visit children and/or relatives and friends in your old age? Do they live close to you? Who visits whom? Does your area have outings for old people, bus trips to see ball games or migrating cranes? Is there an Elderhostel nearby?

Health is self-explanatory and overlaps both finances and food. Do you take responsibility for your health by eating wisely and exercising regularly? Do you trust your doctor or other health professional? What can you do now about the possibility of catastrophic illness? How about investigating homeopathic medicines and naturopathic care? What care do you take of yourself in light of your family illness history? What adjustments are necessary in your lifestyle to cope with the effects of yourself or your partner getting ill?

The subject of food covers more than what we eat and who prepares the food. Where do we shop? Is it based on price or quality or location? Do we take as much care in fixing our own meals as we do for company? Can we afford to go out to eat? Is there a senior diner close by, a meals-on-wheels organization?

Living arrangements bring up a lot of unknowns. Recently a friend moved to a one-level house, saying this was her last move before the nursing home. A good idea, but for how many people is such a move possible? How do I want to live when I am old and what is possible — alone, with family, with women, in a community with other old people, in an intergenerational home? What is financially possible? How much effect do I have on that? Have I visited nursing homes in my area?

Another friend moved halfway across the country to be where her only daughter lives, her second such move. She chose her daughter and grandson over her friends here. How long will this new location last, I wonder? Does one choose family, thinking they have to provide care, or visit a relative at the nursing home, over friends who may or may not be able to provide the care needed?

Considering organizations may seem trivial. Yet belonging has value — to the local YWCA, a church circle, an auxiliary, a professional or advocacy organization. Are the dues affordable on an old age income? Do I belong to any organizations that speak up for the old, such as American Association of Retired Persons, Older Women's League, The Gray Panthers? Which political party best represents my needs in regard to pensions, taxes, retirement and spouse benefits, insurance benefits, housing availability, or health care? Is there a women's center in the area and does it recognize the needs of old women?

Legal matters are an obvious area to pay attention to. Where are our papers? Do we have a will? Have we listed our personal belongings and to whom they go when we die? Have we cleaned out our things — papers, drawers, boxes, closets? Can we make out legal papers ourselves? Who can help us do so?

Alone time might seem an unnecessary reflection for aging women. One hears a lot about the loneliness of old age. Yet we need to find a comfort level between being alone and being with others. Is there a library close by? If we lose our sight, are recordings available? Do we turn on the TV the minute we are alone or make another telephone call? Will we be able to afford long distance calls on our income? Can we be alone part of each day and enjoy that? Is solitude something we are glad for or afraid of?

I've watched my mother literally restored to her former vitality by her move into an apartment complex for "active people, 55 and older." Years of tending her disabled husband kept her socially isolated. Now she has her meals with all the other residents, friends galore, and also the luxury of time alone in her own apartment. She has found the right balance for herself, even in the midst of the pain of putting her husband in a care home and the loss of his presence.

Chores shift and change with aging. Can we change the oil in our car or pay to have someone else do it? Did our partner always take out the garbage or write the thank yous? Are we angry at so much responsibility? Who shovels the walks or calls the building superintendent when the sink stops up? Do we have laundry facilities close and are we able to carry the laundry to and from there? How often do we want to change the sheets on the bed? Are there easier, different ways to accomplish our daily chores?

Relationships always need attention: letters to answer, calls or an amend to make, a problem to face, a talk that can be avoided no longer, a friendship to nurture. Is "the way we've always done it" adequate for old age? or "how it's always been?" What changes can we find the energy for now? Are we open to new friendships and experiences, different patterns?

A group of women reflecting on these things raises enough energy to change the world. Besides making specific plans, the groups of aging women think of who can help and what is the timetable for accomplishing what they choose to do.

"Do not go gentle into that good night," Dylan Thomas (1971, p. 207) wrote, "Old age should burn and rave at close of day; Rage, rage against the dying of the light." We do not have all the time in the world nor is old age something we are powerless over. Under *most* conditions and in many circumstances, women can make choices, reflect and choose, and become more conscious on our way to that "good night."

Chapter 21

Overall Wellness

Two friends of mine, brilliant in human affairs and gifted in leading groups, have an Overall Wellness list of things they think we need to pay attention to.

In no special order, my friends list: (1) improved nutrition; (2) an adequate and consistent exercise program; (3) alone time, to be used for meditation, prayer, renewal; (4) risk (subject of Chapter 22); (5) building a solid support group; (6) getting rid of toxic people in your life; (7) re-creation instead of wreck-creation; (8) knowing what you really love; (9) a love relationship; (10) touch; (11) time management; (12) having a counseling outlet and knowing that you deserve one; (13) maximum of validation and minimum of negative criticism; (14) openness to change and new experiences; (15) fun in your life; (16) art and good music, theater and beauty; (17) clean up your fritters so you have time for all of the above; (18) be free of addictions, in whatever form they come.

I add sleep to my wellness list. When I am short of sleep, my options narrow and I decide life is worthless, everything I am doing is ridiculous and it's all someone else's fault. Both my body and soul require nine hours of sleep out of every 24; it is not depression — I know those symptoms. Sleep is simply the heavenly antidote to my intensity, especially its dreams.

Women in the Women and Aging classes add spiritual practices, social justice work, sharing feelings, humor, time spent outdoors, *yes* escape (through mystery novels, etc.), and playing hooky. Another wellness essential for me is being connected to my three grown daughters, for which I willingly pay a big telephone bill.

To use this Wellness list, add your own important things, check the five you are concentrating on now, and rank them in order of importance. We cannot pay attention to everything at once; we must focus, prioritize and choose. I still hear the voice of my old teacher telling me, as I struggled against the hard work of reducing a list of 12 things to four, that not to choose keeps us in despair.

What to do in some of the areas is obvious. For example: "improved nutrition" includes everything that goes in and out of our mouths, cigarettes, disgorged food for bulimics, vitamins, drugs, sugar.

"Exercise program": daily walking can be our sport, as can following an exercise routine shown on television. But it must not be a spectator sport; we must participate.

"Alone time" is a difficult issue for women, socialized as we are to attend to others and use scraps of leftover time for ourselves. We must take time to be alone, to restore our souls, to do nothing, to sit quietly, resisting the pull of things undone, of culturally-applauded extroversion, of worrying about the ongoing dilemmas of our lives.

Risk and support groups are the subjects of Chapters 22 and 18.

"Getting rid of toxic people" does not mean murder or divorce. It may mean leaving the room when someone is dumping on you. A therapist once asked me what one would do around a spouting volcano. "Get out of the way" was my sensible answer, thus telling myself how to avoid another's spewing anger.

A friend and coworker bombards me with agenda nearly every time I see her, which increases my stress level about a thousand percent. I could ask her not to do this, or set a time each week when she and I could do business, or I could ignore what she says. I want to do something that protects me and does not injure the relationship. Another acquaintance has no boundaries when it comes to helping people. After a meeting in which we've all become much too aware of how overcommitted we are, she'll bring up a new subject, saying "What about . . . ?" My managerial self used to respond, thus feeling responsible for some new job or project; now I listen less attentively and do not respond.

"Re-creation instead of wreck-creation" plays on words to remind us of healthy activity. A good litmus test is this: it doesn't hurt me, doesn't hurt anyone else, and a la the Girl Scouts, leaves this campground better than I found it.

"Knowing what you really love and value" is considered in Chapter 23.

"Having a love relationship" does not necessarily mean a romantic relationship. It can be the intimacy of deep friendship, in which we are safe, affirmed, where we can hear the truth, and speak our own truth with a person whose presence brings us joy and brings us closer to our deepest reality.

"Touch" is central to our lives and we are all starved for it. We live in a culture that has equated touch with sex or the possibility thereof. Our socialized fear and rejection of old people tells us that to touch the old is somehow inappropriate or distasteful.

We need to be conscious and thoughtful about touching others and being touched, with a pat, a hug, a kiss, an arm around a shoulder, hand holding, gentle back rubs, bodies touching as we sit together in meetings, movies or classes. Of course we must be respectful of another's space requirements and our own. We may also need to risk rejection or sexual interpretations and arousal to be loved and touched, to be connected physically as well as emotionally with our human family.

"Time management" is forever on my list of "iffy" areas. In order to do less, I currently try to *not do* one thing on my day's "to do" list. I suffer greatly from over-responsibility! To get started on unfinished projects weighing me down, I practice doing something for five or ten minutes. Writing a quick postcard is easier than the general burden of answering the mail.

"Having a counseling outlet and knowing that you deserve one" is so vital to our health. Counseling is for brave people who want to grow. It does not mean we are crazy or to be pitied, as the old attitude held. We can find good counseling with a professional, a minister or a good friend. It can be co-counseling, as in reevaluation counseling, where two people meet regularly (not social friends) and take turns talking, discharging feelings, listening and encouraging that process.

"Maximum of validation and minimum of negative criticism" is the seed bed for feeling good enough about ourselves to change. We need to be aware of how we validate and/or criticize ourselves, learning to talk back to our vultures.

"Openness to change and new experiences" is self-explanatory,

as is "have art and good music, theater and beauty" in our lives.
(When my youngest daughter Amy, who is an actor, lived in my
town, she encouraged me to take in lots of plays.) "Have fun in
your life" is a little harder to do, brought up as lots of us are with
the standard of the work ethic, the Horatio Alger myth, the Puritan
approach to life. If I do not enjoy life and take time for fun and play
right now, when will I?

"Fritters" does not mean deep-fried batter, but TV watching,
mall-wandering, third-class mail reading, endless telephone talking, endless cleaning and tidying ("picking up and putting down"
as a southern woman I once knew described it), or constant worrying. Yet one person's fritter is another's sanity-saver. I hate to
shop, but have a smart, hardworking acquaintance who finds great
relaxation in shopping trips.

Our addictions are many, not just the obvious ones of food and
mind-altering chemicals, such as alcohol, nicotine, caffeine, and
other drugs. We can be addicted to credit cards, to sex, to busyness,
to work, to a relationship. The adult children-of-alcoholics expert
Rokelle Lerner (1986) says our addictions leave us feeling better
about ourselves or at least numb, as opposed to compulsive behavior and ritual after which we almost always feel worse.

Overall Wellness is not a given. The world does not encourage us
to listen to our inner voice, to reflect on our needs, and to examine
our behaviors and practices to see if they are healthy for us. To
increase our Overall Wellness, we can enlist the help of a friend,
brainstorm solutions with a group, write in our journals, make self-
contracts, bring to consciousness those dimensions of our selves
that make up the lively creative whole woman.

As aging and old women, we can gain power in our lives by
recognizing where we are engaging in self-defeating behavior. We
can claim responsibility for our well-being by reflection—clear,
practical, gentle—wherein we find energy and wisdom for our
lives.

Chapter 22

To Risk or Not To Risk

Risk, Bruce Larson discovered, is a common denominator in mental health. A Presbyterian minister and former head of Faith at Work, a relational theology movement, Larson spent several years on a search funded by a grant from Lilly Endowment, Inc., traveling and interviewing mental health professionals, psychologists, psychiatrists, ministers, therapists, personal growth experts and human potential movement leaders. "Wholeness includes the capacity for choosing creative risk," Larson writes (1978, p. 186). "One of the universal symptoms of mental illness, apparently, is an inordinate need for safety. To live is to risk," Larson discovered, and includes how we "court risk" in our lives, how we overcome fear and try to avoid pain, the need for action, and the ultimate risk.

From my childhood I do not remember hearing or talking about risk. What I remember valuing is certainty, and striving for security — financial, emotional and social. Not until I attended a Values Clarification/Realization workshop in my late 40s, led by Sidney and Suzanne Simon, did I begin to look at the risk in my life. There we separated risk into four categories: physical, emotional, intellectual and spiritual. Then, and on many other occasions, I wrote down nine risks I took in the previous year. This spaded the ground in order to think of nine risks to take in the coming year. (Of course we then rank-ordered these nine, three A's, three B's, and three C's, in order to practice not working on everything at once, ending up not choosing anything.) In risking, the idea is not to jump off the diving board without checking the water in the pool but to reflect on wise, thoughtful risk, and to risk appropriately to one's life.

There was risk in my life, of course, but it wasn't conscious nor would it have been considered worthwhile. Trying out for cheerleader in high school was the ultimate goal for a white, middle-class, small-town girl, growing up in the 1940s when popularity was the main aim of life. I was chosen; had I not been, I would have blamed someone, blamed the selection process, rationalized not being chosen, and been hurt and angry. Such a small thing might have changed my life, instead of affirming the delusion in me that life was only okay as long as I succeeded on the world's terms and that risk could have only one outcome, thereby not being risk.

The idea of risk, taken consciously, contains the possibility of failure, the need to be willing to accept the consequences of one's risk. An anonymous poem says it well:

> To laugh is to risk appearing a fool,
> To weep is to risk appearing sentimental,
> To reach out for another is to risk involvement,
> To expose feelings is to risk exposing your true self,
> To place your ideas, your dreams before the crowd is to risk
>   their loss,
> To love is to risk not being loved in return,
> To live is to risk dying,
> To try is to risk failure,
> But risks must be taken because the greatest hazard in life is to
>   risk nothing,
> Only a person who risks is free.

The one thing I remember most vividly from Erica Jong's *How To Save Your Own Life*, (1977, p. 263) is: ". . . if you don't risk anything, you risk even *more*." Insight is cheap, one is often told, yet when I read that line, it rang true for me and became something I acted on.

C. S. Lewis (1960, p. 169) makes a similar point in *The Four Loves* when he says that keeping a heart safe from love in order to avoid pain leaves that heart "unbreakable, impenetrable, irredeemable." He recommends the risks that accompany the rewards of love, and concludes that "the only place outside of Heaven where you can be perfectly safe from all the dangers and perturbations of love is Hell."

That strong image of the dangers of not taking emotional risks brings up the other side of the coin, the risk of intimacy, letting ourselves be fully known and having in our relationships a deepness that knows no barriers. Emotional risk comes when we say to another, "I'd like to be with you," or "I need your help," or "What do you need from me?" Sometimes I dare to ask my daughters: "Do I call you too much?" I could ask in a meeting where I dominate, "Am I taking too much time, talking too much?" Emotional risk is asking brave questions and getting brave answers.

Sometimes the risk involves being alone. When I am lonely, I am separated from my deepest self, the self that mourns being hidden under convention, fear and busyness. When I recognize this condition, I must risk being alone, cross something off the list, leave things undone, in order to have unscheduled time, or time to "waste."

Intellectual risk is often as simple as turning off the TV, reading a new book, being around people you think are brighter than you, learning new techniques, being open to new content, saying "I don't know."

Physical risk means that we could be hurt. In learning to ride a bicycle we can fall off. Even in walking every day, we risk sore muscles, a rearrangement of our time, possibly less sleep or the need for more, or at least a change in our regular routine.

Spiritual risk may mean reflecting on whether or not the religious training of our childhood is valid for us now; looking at our spiritual practices to see if they are evolving or stagnating, being willing to risk the loss of certainty in order to grow and expand our consciousness. It may mean asking someone to be our spiritual director, to accompany us on that journey of finding our purpose, of acting out of our deepest values, of living with congruence. It requires letting go of certainty.

An old friend wisely reminds me that we are not asked to risk beyond which we cannot live with the consequences; we must not ask more of ourselves than we are ready to pay for. Her words are important to me, since, in my desire to do everything, I sometimes push my risk level too high.

One of the wonders of risking is that it is a sure path to personal power, not power over another but power within one's self. Risk-taking is confidence-building, the results of which hang in with you no matter what happens.

Women are generally rewarded for not taking risks, for behavior that seeks approval from others. One good reason for a connectedness network is that when a risk does not turn out the way you had hoped, you can retreat to the safety and security of supportive friends and not run back to the false security of old behavior, of the patriarchy. Retrenching with people who support us helps avoid people who suggest we "should not have." An illustration of this behavior is that hem lengths go down in hard times, i.e., a retreat to safe behavior.

Your own risk list for this next year may include making an amend, asking someone for time, deciding to move to more age-appropriate housing, cleaning out your stuff, throwing away what you do not need, living on a budget, finding time to nurture your inner life, taking a class, saying no more often, saying yes more often, writing letters instead of telephoning, speaking your truth without fear, guilt or explanations, giving up unhealthy foods, or starting a journal.

A few years ago I took a big risk, consciously and with much trepidation. In order to stop passing for younger than I am and to join my old sisters, I stopped dyeing my hair. I risked my husband's not liking the change and, more, my own confidence based on thinking I was much younger-looking than my age and that I was one of the especially attractive middle-aged women.

It took more than a year for my hair to grow out to the gray-white it is today. I am glad it was a gradual change so I could become used to seeing who I really am, and face some social and self-imposed conventions under which I've lived.

This risk has its price and its rewards, too. I have to learn to cherish who I am at this age, to accept that what I look like is a given and does not define my worth, to give up the deeply-rooted judgment that thin and young-looking are the basis of my self-confidence and self-respect.

In the night, after writing this, I thought of some other risks I've taken — such as joining a Witness for Peace team that went to Nicaragua for eight days in 1984, an action completely at odds with my comfortable, establishment, middle-class background; going to live in Arequipa, Peru, in the summer of 1988 for five weeks, in order to speak Spanish better (I didn't learn much Spanish, hanging around instead with my friend Jean and consoling each other in our culture shock by speaking English); joining a peace march and rally in May of 1982, as my Republican husband was running for his second term as governor of Nebraska. All these risks have changed my life, changed the way I see the world, and given me a broader, deeper, richer life in my becoming-old years.

You have undoubtedly risked more than you think you have: think back to that time you made everyone laugh instead of complaining, that day you changed a habit, that day you got up early to meditate, told someone how much you liked them, took a mental health day off work before you suffered burn-out, made up with a friend, made a new friend, let yourself cry in public, confronted someone who told a sexist/racist/ageist/homophobic joke, wrote a letter to a newspaper, found a way to stop your consumerism, took the time to recycle, listened to and resisted fixing another.

Think of some risks you need and want to take in the next year: throw away old files, let go of a regret or a resentment, make a telephone call, make plans, a step at a time, to do some of those things waiting on your "Someday I'm going to . . ." list.

Experience how good you feel after you do something that is a little scary, that you think you cannot do, that has been nagging at you for a long time. Especially in the becoming-old years, we can restore a sense of personal power by risking, by facing what frightens or intimidates us, by being willing to change and to claim our innate courage.

From an Australian feminist newsletter, *Magdalene*, published in June of 1983, come these stirring words:

> We are strong, we people who are true to ourselves. We have stamina, born of suffering. We travel light because we shed the expectations of others. We travel far because we have glimpsed our destinations. We are determined because our very selves are at stake.

Chapter 23

Tools

Not irreverently I say to Values Clarification/Realization students: "And the word became flesh and dwelt among us." (Growing up in a Christian Science Sunday School, I learned the Bible well.) The analogy of this Christian scripture is, I think, to put action into our beliefs, to move our behavior to the level of our values, to flesh out our deepest beliefs.

Founder of Values Clarification theory and processes, Columbia University professor Louis Raths (1966) said that Values Clarification moves us from our creeds to deeds, closes the gap between what we say we believe and what we actually do, and moves us from our "Ahas" to changed behavior.

Sidney B. Simon has studied and taught Values Clarification and Realization for thirty years, leading seminars and workshops in the U.S. and Europe, and teaching classes at the University of Massachusetts at Amherst. During the last ten years Sidney has been joined by his partner Suzanne Simon.

The Simons cited these differences between Values work and other areas of human growth at a workshop at Amherst in the summer of 1986:

1. We become increasingly decisional, do not drift, and our peer group does not decide for us.

2. There is heavy emphasis on the words and concepts of validation and affirmation.

3. There is a minimum of negative criticism; our self-esteem is in inverse proportion to the amount of negative criticism we've taken in.

4. There is emphasis on non-sexual, therapeutic touch; we pro-

vide safety for each other; our touch is respectful, gentle, and heals, soothes, and validates.

5. Values work is inclusive; others are different, not wrong; there is room for everyone — no cliques, no guru, a minimum of judgment; we are all doing the best we can.

6. In relationships, we emphasize recognition of what we are "pretending not to know;" we ask and answer brave questions; we understand that we create, promote, allow, and abet what occurs in our relationships; we push through fears, get unstuck, and know how to overcome the blocks to change; we face our fears of hurting others and of getting hurt ourselves, again; and we learn how to be allies to those we love.

7. The vital work of forgiveness is begun or continued, an integral component of Values work. We ask how long a sentence do we demand a person serve? We do not forget or condone the injury done us, but at some point let go of past pain through the six-step process of forgiveness (Chapter 24) and live in the present.

8. Values work builds and supports community, using the power of humor, singing, meditations, and providing safety, caring, and confidentiality for each other.

9. We work on pushing our risk level (Chapter 22), knowing that fear is the other side of risk, taking risks with wisdom and skill, which produces exhilaration, increased opportunities and the glorious satisfaction of being in charge of our lives.

10. There is a commitment to overall wellness (Chapter 21) in those crucial places in our lives we need to attend to, to balance the time pressures and remind ourselves we do not have to do our lives alone; we stop fear and panic with the constant discipline of wellness and celebrate our willingness to maintain such a commitment.

11. There is a great deal of self-esteem work, wherein we nourish our uniqueness, not our bizarreness, and learn how we are meant to live.

12. There is a focus on tangible tools in Values work: we do not just talk about our values, we live them.

In my Values Clarification/Realization groups, we keep two running lists — the concepts we are examining and the strategies we exercise to actualize these in our daily lives; that bag of tools we take home from our work. The following are some of those tools:

A. Social scientists Harris Clemes and Reynold Bean (1983) have determined four essential elements of self-esteem, distilled from their years of study and work with students and teachers. They are (1) a sense of uniqueness about ourselves; (2) a connectedness network in our lives; (3) knowledge of choices and the ability to make them; and (4) role models who are doing better than we are. That last does not mean we die of envy. I am convinced that envy is a plumb line to our own possibilities and potential.

B. The Simons quote American psychologist William James who found what he considered three essentials for change: Start immediately, start flamboyantly, and make no exceptions. The seed bed for change is created by increased validation and lowered criticism.

C. As noted in Chapter 17, Mamie Porter (Simon 1978, pp. 74-80) offers three questions that she discovered are all we need to assess and evaluate any situation in our lives. They are: (1) What do I like about what I did? (2) If I were to do it over again, or next time, what would I do differently? (3) And, what help do I need from someone else?

D. Six filters to criticism (Simon, 1978 pp. 65-73) are ways to reduce our judgments of others, condensed in the question: Is it kind, true, necessary? Before offering another criticism, we need to ask ourselves: (1) Is the person in any shape to receive this criticism right now? (2) Am I willing to stick around long enough to help pick up the pieces? (3) How many times has this person heard this criticism before? (4) Can the person do anything about it? (5) Am I positive that none of my own hang-ups, deep-seated psychological needs, hurts, or fears are causing me to make this criticism? (6) Am I sure that what this person needs is another criticism?

E. In *Values and Teaching* (1966) Louis Raths, Merrill Harmin, and Sidney Simon wrote of their pioneering work in how to find values, beyond the obvious values' indicators of beliefs, creeds, goals, morals, aspirations, ideals or activities. People hammer out their values every day; no one hands them to us. A value is something we are passionate about, are willing to be public about, have chosen from among alternatives, are willing to pay the consequences of, have freely chosen, matches our other values, and occurs over and over again in our lives. These seven essential conditions of a value are a solid litmus test to apply to what we say and do.

F. Blocks to change are fear, not knowing alternatives, not using will power appropriately, blaming, not knowing what we really want (values), lack of cooperation skills, low self-esteem, wasting energy in getting the change agent (If I had your money, If you had my partner/childhood/job . . .), and defending the present, rationalizing what is going on in our lives. Recognizing and working on these blocks to change help us get unstuck and push through our fears. An extremely valuable resource is *Getting Unstuck: Breaking Through the Barriers to Change*, Sidney Simon (1988).

There is more, so much more. The main thing to remember is that in Values work, we do not simply talk about what we know and think; we put it into our lives on a daily basis. In Values Realization classes, we read, study and reflect, share with each other, write in our journals, make lists and write letters to ourselves and others, do memory scans and self-inventories, make self-contracts, and have accountability partners.

The work is not self-centered nor narcissistic. Rather it is self-reflective. Personal growth is not an ego trip. It is the work of our lives, enabling us to move out of ourselves to healthy interactions with others and the world beyond ourselves. We do not wait until we have it all together to begin. As someone once paraphrased the words of May Sarton: We take up our anguish and set out.

Those of us aware of how limited our time is and how much affirmative action is necessary to reclaim ourselves and our aging years from the myths of our culture, are especially ready to begin and continue the hard and exciting job of being in charge of our lives. "Time and trouble will tame an advanced young woman," Dorothy L. Sayers (1946) reminds us, "but an advanced old woman is uncontrollable by any earthly force!"

Chapter 24

Our Forgiveness Journey

Forgiveness is essential to good health, especially in the last third of our lives. The burden of resentments, things or people unforgiven, and unfinished business are all too heavy to carry on aging backs. Those people who have done vital unloading through their lives have a wisdom and freedom to be admired. What I know about forgiveness comes from my own experience, Twelve-Step programs, and especially the work of my friends and mentors Suzanne and Sidney Simon.

The idea is: to *free ourselves* from the prison of resentment and regret. The fact that forgiveness affects others is a side blessing. To forgive does not mean to condone evil or bad behavior, just stop hating, let someone off the hook, and find out that "To forgive is to set a prisoner free and discover that prisoner was you."

The main forgiveness work is with one's parents. Issues in our families of origin must be faced. The old resentments do not go away by being ignored; they fester and come out in behaviors that are harder to deal with—in addictions, sideways anger, and the inability to form healthy relationships and partnerships.

Suzanne and Sid Simon (1987, p. 3) write on forgiveness:

> We have all been hurt. The ways in which it happened are beyond counting. Ultimately, it is the way we have chosen to deal with these hurts that has made all the difference in how our lives are working, or not working.

As they describe it, forgiveness is a process, not a one-time mental decision. At first (1) we deny that we have been hurt, saying "It wasn't so bad." Then (2) we move on to self-blame, thinking "If only I'd . . ." done something differently, the bad would not have happened. Later (3) we become victims, whining and passive, trying to ignore the truth that victims are part of a gamey triangle, trading roles with persecutors and rescuers. (4) Indignation blasts us out of victimhood and is an essential stage in the process of forgiving ourselves and others. Now we can get in touch with our anger over what happened to us.

Later (5) we recognize and celebrate that we survived our wounding and that part of our courage and strength comes from surviving that experience or time. (6) At the integration stage, we have finally made peace with our past, the people in our past, and with ourselves. Then we understand and remember that we have forgiven others and have broken the power of the past to disable us.

Forgiveness is not absolving another, nor is it forgetting, wallowing or condoning. It is coming to peace, letting something go, for myself, not for "them." In our forgiveness process, we are able to see the warts of another human being and forgive them; we stop pretending not to know. We recognize that people did the best they could. Until we can forgive our parents, we probably will not be able to forgive ourselves nor have the energy to get on with our lives. Our job is to seek nourishment, insight, and wisdom, so we do not have to repeat the wounds from our past.

Suzanne and Sid (1987, p. 5) conclude:

> We let the experience go because we just don't have to use that event anymore, we don't need it at this point in our journey, we don't need it as our identity. With our increased self-esteem, we have so much more to describe and affirm ourselves about . . . Because we want the joy of being healed, we break the cycle. All of us must climb up to that pinnacle of awareness where we can see that forgiveness is healing.
>
> As a final test, a measure of where you are on your wholeness quest, you might ask yourself these questions: In terms of people who have hurt me: What am I hanging onto? How does it serve me to continue thinking about them in the ways I do? What is the next bold step I need to take for my own inner peace? (The Simons' book, *Forgiveness: How to Make Peace*

With Your Past and Get on With Your Life, 1990, is a splendid guide to this process.)

Theologian Reinhold Niebuhr realized after World War II that "We must finally be reconciled with our foe, lest we both perish in the vicious circle of hatred" (Smedes 1984). How true that is today in so many areas of conflict the world over.

The air went right out of the sails of my self-righteousness a few years ago as I read this paraphrased sentence: In order to bring peace to this world, we must learn to live next door to people with whom we have profound disagreements.

Lewis B. Smedes, professor of ethics at Fuller Seminary in Pasadena, CA, reminds us that "We are seldom merely sinned against; we must confront our own malice" (1985, p. 87).

A marvelous story told by C. S. Lewis illustrates how one must keep working on forgiveness. Troubled most of his life by hurts suffered from a schoolteacher who bullied him, Lewis wrote to a friend shortly before he died:

> Only a few weeks ago, I suddenly realized that I had at last forgiven the schoolmaster. . . . I'd been trying to do it for years and each time I thought I'd done it, I found it had to be attempted again. But this time, I feel sure it is the real thing. (Smedes 1985, p. 88)

Some ways to come to terms with things that continue to cause pain are writing in a journal, talking honestly with a trusted friend, writing letters (and not mailing them) full of everything we ever needed to say to someone living or dead, talking with surrogate parents, or, with a therapist, doing Gestalt chair role-playing.

The quality of aging is enlarged and empowered by a willingness to do the homework, to move through the stages of forgiveness, which ultimately lessens and lifts the burdens of the past and lightens the journey into old age.

If "not being a bitter old woman" is one of my life goals, forgiveness is a sure path to that end. I must start by cleaning the slate with myself—forgiving myself for the idiocies, mistakes, unkindnesses, unreached goals and unattained dreams, the ambivalence and awkwardness of my life.

Marianne Moore wrote: "There never was a war that was not inward: I must fight till I have conquered in myself what causes war." Despite her specific reference to military battles, her words ring true to me, that I may call an internal cease-fire to make peace with my warring selves, those unforgiven selves, inner and outer.

Chapter 25

Before the Casket Closes

At some point in our lives, we may wonder how many years we have left to live, and how we want to spend those years. Things I've always wanted to do or hoped I'd do someday come to my mind. At 59, what I want to do before I die becomes a matter of immediate concern, rather than an eventual possibility.

Writer May Sarton (1984, p. 92) says in *At Seventy: A Journal*,

> So what is the inward order that makes it possible to shut out the chaos around me as I sit here? Perhaps a strong sense of what my priorities are — first friends, then work, then the garden. If I died suddenly, how bitterly I should regret work undone, friends unanswered.

Of myself I ask: "What do I not want to regret not having done when I die?" A yellowed newspaper column I've saved ends with this poignant cry: "Oh, God, don't let me die bewildered!" Jim Moore, a writer for the *Lincoln Journal*, uses the phrase "before the coffin lid lowers" as his way of finding out what he needs to do before he dies.

At the age of 60, theologian Robert McAfee Brown (1988, p. 8) writes that he resents

> the fraility of my tenure among all that I have come to love. I want it to go on. I want to keep renewing acquaintances with old friends, deepening acquaintances with new friends . . . to see Chile free of Pinochet and my exiled friends able to return there . . . to see a birch grove, destroyed by winter ice and my over-enthusiastic pruning, reborn from the stumps. I want more years with my wife and children . . . to know all the

Beethoven string quartets well . . . to be reassured that political prisoners will be freed . . . I want to be here when Third World peoples begin to get their fair shake. *I don't want my tenure among such things to be so frail.* And it is.

He asks if "Time. My enemy" could be his friend and responds,

Maybe. We need not wait until we are nearing 60 to face these questions and search for answers. The sooner one begins to face them the more time there will be to live out the affirmations toward which they point.

"Solution," McAfee Brown writes in specific detail, is to "stop wasting the already precious moments griping about the passage of time, and get on with the affirmation of the present moments as grace-filled."

There is a marvelous exercise that moves one into some heartfelt figuring about the rest of one's life. The first step is to choose the age at which you think you will die, taking into account genes, lifestyle, and zest for life. This exercise is *not* a self-fulfilling prophecy, and can be changed every day. Now draw a line across a sheet of paper and write your birth year on the left of the line, the year you think you will die on the right side, and your current age at the appropriate place in-between. Next draw a half-circle below the line, from your birth date to your current age; in that space or "net," write as many of your life experiences and mileposts as you can think of in a few minutes. This half-circle represents every moment you have breathed, everything you have ever felt, every person you have known, every moment of your life stored in your brain cells. In my recollecting, I list children, towns, memorable experiences, habits, schools, studies, churches, friends, vacations, houses, groups, pets, family members, precious memories, favorite places, turning points, fun times, grievings, anything I can think of in a few minutes.

"If I could have filled my net differently, I would have . . ." is a subject you may want to write about for a few minutes. This is hard work and, although it is often depressing to face one's regrets, it may uncover things to include on your "I don't want to regret not having done" list.

Draw another half-circle, above the line, this one a rainbow, from the point of your current age to the fantasized date of your death. This represents the years we figure we have left to live. In whatever time I have left, it is good to think about what I want to do or what I do not want to leave undone, by putting some of the "Someday, I'll . . ." things at the top of that list.

My wise, thoughtful friend Adrian writes to me: "You do push me to be more definite with what to do with the next 10 years of my life. Now that I am 70, I have to plan how to be 80 and what I may be forced to let go of." Christopher Morely said, "If everyone was given five minutes warning before sudden death, every telephone booth would be occupied by people trying to call up other people to say, 'I love you.'"

In a different vein, Clark University teacher Pam Wright (1988, p. 90), in her article "Living With Death As A Teacher," asks "What would you do with your life if you knew you had a year to live? What would give you joy? Ask a lot of people. Eventually someone will say, 'But if we all did that, everything would fall apart.' Exactly."

My list changes from year to year yet some things stay on it for a long time. For no reason other than solidarity, I want to speak Spanish fluently before I die. Some people want to plant a garden, make up with a friend, forgive a parent, go whitewater rafting, be closer to a child, have more time for solitude or play; some want to spend a month at the beach and others want to be more involved in helping others, fly the Concorde to Paris, dye their hair, learn to downhill ski, get their GED, or have a glorious love affair.

To keep on focusing, prioritizing, and rearranging our priorities, we can take a list of 12 things that we want to do and mark four As, four Bs, and four Cs; then take one from the A list and work out the steps needed to reach that goal, when it will be carried out and who can help. All of this puts substance and action into our dreams, even our longing to take time to reflect on our dreams.

Toni Morrison (1977, p. 149) writes of Pilate in *Song of Solomon*:

When she realized what her situation in the world was and would probably always be she threw away every assumption she had learned and began at zero. First off, she cut her hair. That was one thing she didn't want to think about anymore.

Then she tackled the problem of trying to decide how she wanted to live and what was valuable to her.

Carolyn Heilbrun (1988, Sept. 4, p. 25) notes, "The point is not the joys of old age, in which I do not, in a general way, believe. The point is, probably, death, and the intensity of knowledge it brings." She speaks of women who have "re-created themselves when closure might have seemed almost upon them." Heilbrun (1988, p. 131) also cautions that

> those with some assured place and pattern in their lives, with some financial security—are in danger of choosing to stay right where we are, to undertake each day's routine, and to listen to our arteries hardening. I do not believe that death should be allowed to find us seated comfortably in our tenured positions. . . . Instead, we should make use of our security, our seniority, to take risks, to make noise, to be courageous, to become unpopular. . . .
>
> Neither rocking on a porch, nor automatically offering her services as cook and housekeeper and child watcher, nor awaiting another chapter in the heterosexual plot, the old woman must be glimpsed through all her disguises which seem to preclude her right to be called woman. She may well for the first time be woman herself.

A serendipitous moment came during the last series of Women and Aging classes I led. A woman read aloud the Jenny Joseph poem (Martz 1987, p. 1) entitled "Warning" that opens with the well-known line, "When I am an old woman I shall wear purple," another read Betty Mills' (1987) takeoff on "When I am an Old Woman," that begins, "I shall wear mostly jeans and T-shirts that say outrageous things." Spontaneously, I suggested that we write for a few minutes on "When I am an old woman, I shall . . ." The results were fun, tender, wise, silly, thought-provoking, heartrending, energy-providing.

One woman wrote "Now that I am over seventy, I will no longer worry—what people think of me, about wasting my time, about money, too much about my health and weight, about the world falling apart if I just say no once in a while." Another said, in great good humor, ". . . I shall refrain from giving away life's big secrets and sit back and smugly watch my kids figure it out for themselves.''

Others said: When I am an old woman, I will . . .

- not care if anyone sees my cat drink iced tea from my glass.
- go to church and leave afterwards without fellowshipping.
- wonder what I did wrong . . . and not hold my stomach in and make airline reservations at the last minute and not know my return date.
- take my grandchildren on pro-choice marches . . . go to Nepal with Rosemary.

I wrote,

> When I am an old woman, I'll have no fights except those that have a chance of changing something; And I'll go to the movies sometimes without doing the supper dishes. I'll go naked in my house and on secluded beaches and learn to love my aging heavy body. I'll do dances and meditations at the full moon and other witchly things. And know what my dreams are saying and paint at my kitchen table.

By writing these tender things, by making lists of risks I need to take, from musing on What I Want Not to Regret Not Having Done, I find ways to change, to accept, to choose and make decisions, to act on what I want in the years I may have left to live.

Chapter 26

Celebration

My dear old buddy Joyce is a celebrator of everything. Coming home late in the afternoon and in low spirits on my birthday one year, I found the front door plastered with wise and pithy sayings Joyce had gathered from friends and acquaintances, all written to and about me. In the time we have been friends, I have not known her to miss a birthday, a wedding, an anniversary, a graduation, a retirement, or any reason for letting someone know they are loved and cherished. I have learned from Joyce much of what I know about ritual, tradition, celebration, about marking events in my life and those of my family and friends.

Another learning and growing place is with a small group of women friends as we get together on the solstices, equinoxes and the four times that cross those turnings of the earth. We read, talk and reflect, and do small rituals that connect us with the seasons and the rhythmns of our lives. In the peace movement, we come together to listen to one another, to have potluck suppers, sharing simple food and time. In Quaker meeting, we listen in silence together, and sometimes speak of our deepest needs and longings and leadings. I take late afternoon walks with a friend and we both find places in our lives to celebrate, to affirm each other's wisdom.

In all these forms of celebration, I learn to hold still, to mark an occasion, to cherish a friend, to acknowledge a span of time, to honor an accomplishment. My youngest daughter has always insisted I mark her opening nights of plays with a special gift. I am glad for this push from Amy because now I think of Annie's getting her first nursing job, Mary's recovery from illness and completion of a huge editing job, as times in our lives worth a telephone call, a present, or an acting out of joy and gratitude.

Surely no less a time for celebration is that of aging. In groups of women reflecting on our own aging, we list the compensations of age and aging. We write poems and read them to the group. We go around the table and speak one word to describe our feelings about something. We rejoice in the little things of our lives and celebrate each other's changes and choices. Not all our words represent "positive thinking," nor are they meant to. Sometimes we poke fun at ourselves, our humor is wry, our truth about ourselves both sentimental and bittersweet.

We do celebrate our lives as we take a hard look at them, make changes and plans for change, talk about our fears and hopes, help one another overcome our culture's denigration of old women, and our own internalized criticism of ourselves. We celebrate by getting together to talk, to listen, to have fun, to eat a meal, to work on a project, to figure out how to get something done, to be bawdy and irreverent, to study, reflect and grow, to comfort and commiserate, to wonder and applaud.

Our celebrations are both tiny and grand. We celebrate forgiving an old hurt just as much as we celebrate a birthday, or our own coming into old age. We do not wait just for traditional occasions to celebrate, to get out the good dishes, to wear our best perfume. A normal pap smear is cause for celebration as an irregular one is cause for reflection and action.

I have long kept an old newspaper article, now nearly unreadable, titled "What Are We Waiting For?" by Ann Wells of Laguna Niguel, California, in which she talks of her sister's unexpected death. She and her brother-in-law were picking out clothes to take to the mortician when they found an exquisite silk slip, handmade and trimmed with lace, which the sister had bought for a pretty penny on a trip to New York eight or nine years prior to her death. "She was saving it for a special occasion," the husband told Ann. "Well, I guess this is the occasion," he said, both in sorrow and despair. "Don't ever save anything for a special occasion," he told her. "Every day you're alive is a special occasion."

Ann Wells writes, after the funeral,

> It's those little things left undone that would make me angry if I knew that my hours were limited. Angry because I put off seeing good friends whom I was going to get in touch with — someday. Angry because I hadn't written certain letters that I

intended to write — one of these days. Angry and sorry that I didn't tell my husband and daughter often enough how much I truly love them. I'm trying very hard not to put off, hold back, or save anything that would add laughter and luster to our lives.

I am constantly amazed at the power and energy of women to get together to nurture one another, to shore up one another's courage, to laugh and cry together, to mourn and to celebrate, and to do it as a community that cares about and is committed to one another. We listen to the stories of one another's lives and respond.

In our aging groups, we keep ongoing lists of life-enhancing behaviors and situations — such as laughing and crying, hobbies, intimacy, causes, solitude, mammograms, telephone visits, hot baths, letting go of guilt, not criticizing ourselves or others, sleep, singing, reading, continuing to learn. A list of 100 such life-enhancers can be made in a matter of minutes.

Concurrently, we keep a list of finite-accepting behaviors, to remind ourselves, against the culture's myth, that we do not live forever. Some items on this list include writing a will, going to funerals, the loss of a driver's license, spending time with old people regularly, hospice work, changes in sleep patterns, eyeglass strength, height of heels, holding power of kidneys, reading and writing obituaries, taking a class with other women on aging issues, slowing down, cleaning out our accumulations.

We both celebrate and find energy for our lives and learn to balance our aspirations and longings with our limitations and failures. We celebrate by dancing, eating, drinking, touching, looking, listening, talking, being silent together, being present to one another, with our eyes and bodies, our hands and our heads. We walk with one another and sometimes sit facing one another. We tell each other our deepest truths and listen to music and write stories together.

The resources for this journey together into old age range from books we recommend to each other to our own experiences and those of other women. Such empowering books include Monica Sjöö and Barbara Mor's, *The Great Cosmic Mother: Rediscovering the Religion of the Earth* (1987, p. 430), in which they write the prophetic words, "Now is the time to make again sacred our experience"; Riane Eisler's *The Chalice & The Blade, Our History, Our Future*, called "a major breakthrough" by Barbara Walker; and *The Politics of Women's Spirituality*, edited by Charlene Spretnak.

We also reflect on such realities as those described below by Human Services Administrator Kit Boesch. In an article about a program for those at high risk for unemployment, welfare, and other dependency, Boesch (1990) wrote:

> Front line case workers, often well intentioned, get into a head-patting stage generally accompanied by words like, "There, there now. Things will get better. You just need to improve yourself. Have a little initiative." To a single woman with three children under the age of eight, who has no GED and can't find food for tonight's meal, those comments don't mean squat. They're empty and meaningless. How much more initiative can she have than holding down two part-time, minimum wage jobs?

Among other examples of the recorded experience of women is an article, "Learning from Experience," in the magazine, *Woman of Power* (1989), reporting on the plenary session on older women at Forum 1985, the nongovernmental segment of the UN Conference on Women. Beginning with Meridel LeSueur's "I am luminous with age" from the poem "Rites of Ancient Ripening" (p. 62), the voices of aging women the world over speak from these pages, as does the "Agenda for the Future: Suggestions for Action Regarding Older Women" (p. 64). Some of the 14 suggestions are: (1) Organize older women to become advocates to promote their own interests and to provide needed services; (2) educate women of all ages about the realities of aging to encourage social and economic independence in their later years; (3) promote those people for government service who will act as advocates for older women in the development of policies and programs; (4) publicize the positive aspects of aging, the contributions older women make to society, and individual female models of positive aging; (5) train older women to have marketable skills; (6) provide support systems for ailing elderly women and for their family caregivers; (7) arrange opportunities for intergenerational experiences; (8) insure appropriate and accessible health care services.

To bring closure to several weeks together, one group of aging women each contributed a line to this honest, funny, powerful poem about our aging.

Aging Is . . .

Proof that I am still alive
Not worrying about a clean house
Being less self-conscious
Twenty minutes on the telephone with grandchildren singing
    their songs
Laughing with old friends
Crying with old friends
Being able to laugh at myself
Not taking myself too seriously
Taking my life seriously
Singing and dancing for the joy of being alive
Having fond memories
Choices—selecting and eliminating what I want to do
Exciting because I've made it
Having some specific aches and pains I can complain about
Wearing Birkenstocks in the winter
Not always being on someone else's schedule
Dressing comfortably
Sharing affection anytime, anyplace, without being embar-
    rassed
Realizing death is a big part of life
Being able to give advice
Letting go of lots of different things
Learning for the fun of it
Having time for new and deeper relationships
Having time to listen
Having time to watch sunrises and sunsets
Hearing the geese and the cranes
Victory!

Epilogue

Quite some time after I finished writing this book, my mother died of cancer, three months before turning 86, in bed in my sister's house. Ann and I held her hands, and Ann's husband urged us to keep talking to her, after she'd not caught a breath for two minutes. He was right; we need to keep talking, for her spirit and ours.

Her dying taught me that dying is no easy thing, even as we know death is merciful. She struggled in that process, through both profound and physical issues. She took no chemotherapy nor radiation, nor any IVs. Hospice managed my mother's home care and home-health aids did round-the-clock shifts. It was all loving, dignified, professional, hard and exhausting and grief-laden.

I want to go screaming away from my life, from my greed and envy and childishness and tiredness, from my own mortality and aging. Surely there is some great adventure yet, in the 20 years of my life from 60 to 80.

Growing old seems entirely unmanageable at this moment. Dying is no small subject, as living is not either. Our human life-span is short and often sweet. How extraordinary I am finding the effect of its last years and its ending.

Bibliography

Ault, Robert (1986). "Elizabeth Layton" by Lucy Lippard in *Women and Aging: An Anthology by Women*, edited by: Jo Alexander, Debi Berrow, Lisa Domitrovich, Margarita Donnelly, Cheryl McLean, Corvallis, OR. Calyx Books.

Auden, W. H. (1975). *Collected longer poems*. New York: Vintage.

Bass, Ellen. (1986, November). Courage. [Poem for the November page.] *Syracuse Cultural Workers calendar*. Syracuse Cultural Workers, 126 Intervale Road, Burlington, VT 05401.

Bauer, Jan. (1982). *Alcoholism and women: The background and the psychology*. Toronto: Inner City Books.

Becker, Ernest. (1973). *The Denial of death*. New York: Free Press.

Boesch, Kit. (1990, Summer). Home. *Women's Journal-Advocate*, Lincoln, NE.

Bolen, Jean Shimoda. (1990). A talk at "Women's Wisdom" retreat at Feathered Pipe Ranch, Helena, MT.

Brown, Robert McAfee. (March-April 1988). "Making Friends with Time," *Faith at Work* magazine, Faith at Work, Columbia, MD.

Burton, Gabrielle. (1972). *I'm running away from home but I'm not allowed to cross the street; a primer of women's liberation*. Pittsburgh: Know Publishing.

Charland, Paula. (May 20, 1987). "Dispelling Old Myths," from an interview with Marcy Adelman, Editor of *Long Time Passing: Lives of Older Lesbians*. *Bay Window*, New England Gay and Lesbian newspaper.

Clemes, Harris and Bean, Reynold. (1983). *How to raise children's self-esteem*. San Jose: Ohaus.

Copper, Baba. (1986). "Voices: On Becoming Old Women," in *Women and Aging: An Anthology by Women*, edited by: Jo Alexander, Debi Berrow, Lisa Domitrovich, Margarita Donnelly, Cheryl McLean, Corvallis, OR, Calyx Books.

Dillard, Annie. (1989). *The writing life*. New York: Harper & Row.

Eisler, Riane. (1988). *The Chalice & The Blade, Our History, Our Future*. San Francisco: Harper & Row.

Ellwood, Gracia Fay. (1988). *Batter my heart*. (Pendle Hill Pamphlet No. 282.) Wallingford, PA: Pendle Hill Publications.

Fields, Rick. (1984). *Chop wood, carry water; a guide to finding spiritual fulfillment in everyday life*. Los Angeles: Tarcher.

Gaines, Joan. (1987, July-August). *OWL* (Older Women's League) *Observer*.

Gault, Jan. (1983). *Free time: Making your leisure count*. New York: Wiley Press. Quoted in Churchman, Deborah. (1985, July 15). How to liven up your leisure: Plan your spare moments — don't fritter them away. *Christian Science Monitor*, p. 26.

Guggenbuhl-Craig, Adolf. (1987). "Aging: Old Bottles, New Wine" seminar announcement, C. G. Jung Foundation, New York.

Healey, Shevy. (1986). "Growing to Be an Old Woman; Aging and Ageism" in *Women and Aging: An Anthology by Women*, edited by: Jo Alexander, Debi Berrow, Lisa Domitrovich, Margarita Donnelly, Cheryl McLean, Corvallis, OR. Calyx Books.

Heilbrun, Carolyn. (1988, Sept. 4). Women writers: Coming of age. *New York Times Book Review*, pp. 1, 23, 25.

Heilbrun, Carolyn. (1988). *Writing a woman's life*. New York: W. W. Norton.

Henig, Robin Marantz. (1988, January 17). Older, wiser and stronger: Feminists look ahead. [A review of *Ourselves, growing older*]. *Book World (Washington Post)*, p. 4.

Horney, Karen. (1945). *Our inner conflicts*. New York: W. W. Norton.

James, Henry. (1980). Aug. 21, 1913, "Letter to Hugh Walpole," p. 654:7 *Familiar Quotations*, John Bartlett, edited by Emily Morrison Beck, Little, Brown & Co., Boston.

Kano, Susan. (1989). *Making peace with food: Freeing yourself from the diet/weight obsession*. New York: Harper & Row.

Jong, Erica. (1977). *How To Save Your Own Life.* New York: Holt, Rinehart and Winston.

Kilbourne, Jean. (1981). *Killing us softly; Advertising's image of women.* Cambridge, MA: Cambridge Documentary Films.

Kilbourne, Jean. (1982). *Calling the shots; The advertising of alcohol.* Cambridge, MA: Cambridge Documentary Films.

Kilbourne, Jean. (1987). *Still killing us softly.* Cambridge, MA: Cambridge Documentary Films.

Kolbenschlag, Madonna. (1988). *Lost in the land of Oz: The Search for identity and community in American Life.* New York: Harper & Row.

Kopp, Sheldon. (1972). *If you meet the Buddha on the road, kill him; The pilgrimage of psychotherapy patients.* New York: Bantam.

Kuhn, Maggie. (1984). *Chop wood, carry water.* Los Angeles: Jeremy P. Tarcher.

Larson, Bruce. (1978). *The Meaning and mystery of being human.* Waco, TX: Word Books.

Learning from experience. (1989, Summer). *Woman of Power,* pp. 62-65. Report prepared by American Association for International Aging, Washington, D.C., 1986. Charlotte W. Conable, Project Coordinator.

Lerner, Rokelle. (Speaker). (1986). *Journey Through Shame* [cassette recording of an address to the Houston, Texas U.S. Journal Conference in 1986].

Lewis, C. S. (1960). *The four loves.* New York: Harper & Row.

Lippard, Lucy. (1986). "Elizabeth Layton," in *Women and Aging: An Anthology by Women,* edited by: Jo Alexander, Debi Berrow, Lisa Domitrovich, Margarita Donnelly, Cheryl McLean, Calyx Books, Corvallis, OR.

Macdonald, Barbara. (1987, July). A movement of old lesbians. [Keynote address at the West Coast Old Lesbian Conference and Celebration in April 1987.] *Off our backs,* pp. 3 & 15.

Magdelene, June, 1983, Australian feminist newsletter.

Martz, Sandra, ed. (1987). *When I am an old woman, I shall wear purple; an anthology of short stories and poetry.* Manhattan Beach, CA: Papier-Maché Press.

Mills, Betty. (1987, July-August). When I am an old woman. *Woman's Journal-Advocate*, Lincoln, NE.

Mitchell, Pam. (1990, June). Ronnie Gilbert: We are either going to make it together or we're not going to make it. *The Progressive*, pp. 32-35.

Montagu, Ashley, (1981). *Growing Young*. New York: McGraw-Hill.

Morrison, Toni. (1977). *Song of Solomon*. New York: Knopf.

Olsen, Tillie. (1978). *Silences*. New York: Delacorte/Seymour Lawrence.

Olson, Hertha. (Nov.-Dec. 1987). "A Piece Is Missing," p. 52, *Life Lines* magazine, The Lincoln Area Agency on Aging, Lincoln, NE.

Piercy, Marge. (1982). "If They Come in the Night" from *Circles on the Water*, New York, Borzoi Books, Alfred A. Knopf, Inc.

Pipher, Mary (1988). *Hunger pains: The American women's tragic quest for thinness*. Lincoln, NE: Barking Gator Press.

Preston, Caroline. (1987). Empowerment in aging. *Source*. [Quoted in *OWL Observer*, 1987, July-August]. Seattle: Church Council of Greater Seattle.

Raths, Louis, Harmin, Merrill and Simon, Sidney. (1966). *Values and teaching*. Columbus, Ohio: Charles E. Merrill.

Reis, Patricia. (1988, Winter). The dark goddess. *Woman of Power*, pp. 24-27, 82.

Rich, Adrienne. (1977). *Working it out*. New York: Pantheon.

Rich, Adrienne. (1985). *Moonflower, a book of affirmations*. Freedom, CA: The Crossing Press.

Rich, Cynthia. (1990, March-April). Ageism and the politics of beauty. *Broomstick: Options for women over forty*, San Francisco, pp. 6-10.

Rubin, Ted. (1976). *Love me, love my fool*. New York: McKay.

Ruddick, Sara and Daniels, Pamela. (1977). *Working it out: 23 women writers, artists, scientists and scholars talk about their lives and work*. New York: Pantheon.

Sarton, May. (1984). *At seventy, a journal*. New York: W. W. Norton.

Sayers, Dorothy. (1946). Are women human? *Unpopular opinions*. London: Gallancz, pp. 106-115.

Schaef, Anne Wilson. (1987). *When society becomes an addict.* San Francisco: Harper & Row.

Scott-Maxwell, Florida. (1979) *The measure of my days.* New York: Penguin Books.

Simon, Sidney B. (1978). *Negative criticism and what you can do about it.* Niles, IL: Argus Communications.

Simon, Sidney B. and Simon, Suzanne. (1987). Forgiveness: Healing the hurt. *Realizations* (Values Realization Institute), pp. 3-5.

Simon, Sidney B. (1988). *Getting unstuck: Breaking through the barriers to change.* New York: Warner Books.

Simon, Sidney B. and Simon, Suzanne. (1990). *Forgiveness: How to make peace with your past and get on with your life.* New York: Warner Books.

Simon, Sidney B. and Suzanne. (1986, Summer). Values Clarification-Realization workshop, Amherst, MA.

Sjöö, Monica and Mor, Barbara. (1987). *The great cosmic mother: Rediscovering the religion of the earth.* New York: Harper & Row.

Smedes, Lewis B. (1984). *Forgive and forget: Healing the hurts we don't deserve.* New York: Harper & Row.

Smedes, Lewis B. (1985, August). Forgiveness: love's healing miracle. [Condensation of *Forgive and forget. . .*] *Reader's Digest,* pp. 85-89.

Spretnak, Charlene. (1982). *The Politics of Women's Spirituality,* Garden City, NY, Anchor Books, Doubleday.

Starhawk. (1982). *Dreaming the Dark: Magic, Sex and Politics,* pp. 37, 63, Boston, Beacon Press.

Stassinopoulos, Arianna. (Nov. 4, 1984). "Dr. Jonas Salk's Formula for the Future: Courage, Love, Forgiveness," New York, *Parade* magazine.

Stoddard, Sally. (1990). "Women, Language, and Power," paper presented at The Unitarian Church, Lincoln, NE.

Strouse, Jean. (1980). *Alice James, a biography.* Boston: Houghton-Mifflin.

Sun magazine. (September, 1986). #130, "US/Readers Write About Regrets," pp. 18-19, Chapel Hill, NC. The Sun Publishing Co.

Svitil, Torene. (1990, January-February). "Why older is better than younger," *Utne Reader*, p. 74, Minneapolis, MN, Lens Publishing Co.

Szacz, Thomas. (1973). *The Second Sin*, New York: Doubleday & Co.

Tennyson, Alfred Lord. *In Memoriam*, 1850, "Prologue" p. 78, st. 5.

Thomas, Dylan. (1971). *The Poems of Dylan Thomas*. New York: New Directions.

Thompson, Becky (1988, Fall). Women's hunger and feeding ourselves. *Woman of Power Magazine* (Issue 11), pp. 78-79, 82-84.

Thone, Ruth. (May 26, 1990). "This Moment Most Valuable of All," *Lincoln Star*.

Twarogowski, Janet. (1990). *Support groups: It doesn't have to be you alone against the world*. Hadley, MA: Values Realization Institute. P.O. Box 230, Hadley, MA 01035.

Ulanov, Ann Belford. (1986). *Picturing God*. Cambridge, MA: Cowley Publications.

Walker, Barbara. (1982). Inside cover, Eisler, Riane, *The Chalice & The Blade, Our History, Our Future*, San Francisco: Harper & Row.

White, Maxine. (1990, June). Growing old disgracefully. *Matrix* (Santa Cruz, CA), pp. 4-5.

Women and aging; an anthology by women (1986). Edited by Jo Alexander, Debi Berrow, Lisa Domitrovich, Margarita Donnelly, and Cheryl McLean. Corvallis, OR: Calyx Books.

Wright, Pam. (1988, Winter). Living with death as a teacher. *Woman of Power*, pp. 12-13, 90.

Reading List

Some of my favorite books and publications on the subject of Women and Aging are:

Adelman, Marcy, editor, *Long Time Passing: Lives of Older Lesbians*, Alyson Publications, Boston, MA, 1986.

Alexander, Jo, et al., editors, *Women and Aging, an anthology by Women*, Calyx Books, Corvallis, OR, 1986.

Andrews, Elsie Marion, *Facing and Fulfilling the Later Years*, Pendle Hill Pamphlet 157, Pendle Hill Publications, Wallingford, PA, 1968.

Bell, Marilyn, editor, *Women as Elders: The Feminist Politics of Aging*, Harrington Park Press, New York, London, 1986.

Billig, Nathan, *To be Old and Sad, Understanding Depression in the Elderly*, Lexington Books, D.C. Heath and Co., Lexington, MA and Toronto, 1987.

Chapkis, Wendy, *Beauty Secrets: Women and the Politics of Appearance*, South End Press, Boston, 1986.

Copper, Baba, *Over the Hill, Reflections on Ageism Between Women*, The Crossing Press, Freedom, CA, 1988.

de Beauvoir, Simone, *Coming of Age*, Putnam, 1972.

de Beauvoir, Simone, *A Very Easy Death*, Pantheon, 1985.

Doress, Paul Brown, & Siegal, Diana Laskin and the Midlife and Older Women Book Project in cooperation with The Boston Women's Health Book Collective, *Ourselves, Growing Older*, Touchstone/Simon and Schuster, 1987.

Eisler, Riane, *The Chalice and The Blade: Our History, Our Future*, Harper & Row, NY, 1987.

Field, Joanna, *A Life of One's Own*, J. P. Tarcher, Inc., 1981.

Fields, Rick, et al., editors, *Chop Wood, Carry Water*, (aging chapter) Jeremy P. Tarcher, Inc., Los Angeles, St. Martin's Press, New York, 1984.

Fischer, M.F.K., *Sister Age*, Knopf, New York, 1983.

Heilbrun, Carolyn G., *Writing a Woman's Life*, W. W. Norton & Co., New York, London, 1988.

Jacobs, Ruth Harriet, *Older Women: Surviving and Thriving: A Manual for Group Leaders*, Family Service America, Milwaukee, 1987.

Kolbenschlag, Madonna, *Lost in the Land of Oz: The Search for Identity and Community in American Life*, Harper & Row, 1988.

Larrain, Virginia, *Timeless Voices*, Celestial Arts, Millbrae, CA, 1978.

Luce, Gay Gaer, *Your Second Life, Vitality and Growth in Middle and Later Years*, Merloyd Lawrence Book, Dell Publishing Co., 1979.

Luke, Helen M., *Old Age*, Parabola Books, New York, 1987.

MacDonald, Barbara, with Cynthia Rich, *Look Me in the Eye, Old Women, Aging and Ageism*, Spinsters, Ink, San Francisco, 1983.

Morton, Nelle, *The Journey Is Home*, Beacon Press, 1985.

Murphy, Carol, *Milestone 70*, Pendle Hill Pamphlet 287, Pendle Hill Publications, Wallingford, PA, 1989.

Martz, Sandra, editor, *When I Am an Old Woman I Shall Wear Purple*, Papier-Maché Press, Manhattan Beach, CA, 1987.

Nouwen, Henri J. M., *Aging* Image Books, Doubleday & Co., Inc., Garden City, NY, 1976.

Painter, Charlotte & Valois, Pamela, writer, photographer, *Gifts of Age*, Chronicle Books, 1985.

Penelope, Julia, *Speaking Freely: Unlearning the Lies of the Fathers' Tongues*, The Athene Series, Pergamon Press, Elmsford, New York, 1990.

Ruddick, Sara, and Pamela Davis, editors, *Working It Out, 23 Women Writers, Artists, Scientists & Scholars Talk About Their Lives and Work*, Pantheon Books, New York, 1977.

Sarton, May, *As We Are Now*, W. W. Norton & Co., New York, London, 1973.

Sarton, *At 70*, W. W. Norton & Co., NY, London, 1984.

Sarton, *Recovering*, W. W. Norton & Co., NY, London, 1980.

Schoenfielder, Lisa and Barb Wieser, *Shadow on a Tight Rope: Writings by Women on Fat Oppression*, Spinsters/Aunt Lute, San Francisco, 1983.

Scott-Maxwell, Florida, *The Measure of My Days*, Penguin Books, 1979.

Sjöö, Monica, & Barbara Mor, *The Great Cosmic Mother: Rediscovering the Religion of the Earth*, Harper & Row, 1987.

√Spretnak, Charlene, editor, *The Politics of Women's Spirituality*, Anchor Press, 1982.

Tisdale, Sallie, *Harvest Moon: Portrait of a Nursing Home*, Henry Holt & Co., 1987.

Ulanov, Ann Belford, *Picturing God, (chapter) Aging: On the Way to One's End*, Cowley Publications, 1986.

Viorst, Judith, *Forever Fifty and Other Negotiations*, Simon and Schuster, NY, 1989.

Walker, Barbara, *The Crone*, Harper and Row, San Francisco, 1985.

Wolf, Naomi, *The Beauty Myth: How Images of Beauty Are Used Against Women*, Wm. Morrow and Co., Inc., New York, 1991.

Some of my favorite magazines are:

Woman of Power, a magazine of Feminism, spirituality, and politics, Box 827, Cambridge, MA, 02238.

The Sun, a magazine of ideas, 107 N. Roberson St., Chapel Hill, NC 27516.

Z Magazine, 150 West Canton St., Boston, MA 02118.

Broomstick, By, For, and About Women Over Forty, 3543 18th St., San Francisco, CA 94110.

Index

Addiction, 107,110
Advertising, women's portrayal by, 20-21
Advocacy, 134
Affirmative action, *xiii,* 79,120
Ageism
 in advertising, 20
 definition, 27
 internalized, 15-16,53-55,63
 semantics of, 25-28
Aging
 celebration of, 131-135
 childlike traits of, 41-45
 cultural attitudes towards, 20, 61-63
 definition, 27
 disgracefully (fortune of), 14
 "gracefully", 13-17
 grief of, 57-59
 mystique, *xi*
Alcohol, advertising of, 20
Alcoholics Anonymous (AA), 95-96
Alcoholism and Women: The Background and the Psychology (Bauer), 96
American Association of Retired Persons, 105
Anger
 death and dying-related, 71-73,74
 functions of, 74
Anxiety, death and dying-related, 73-75

Ball, Lucille, 23
Bolk, Louise, 43
Bombeck, Erma, 24
Brainstorming, 97,110
Bridge clubs, 96
Brown, McAfee, 125,126

Cather, Willa, 82
Celebration, 131-135
Chalice and the Blade, Our History, Our Future, The (Eisler), 134
Change, 119
 obstacles to, 120
 openness towards, 107-110
Childlike traits, 41-45
Christopher, Jim, 96
Church membership, 65-67
Clark, Septima, 59
Cosby, Gordon, 22-23
Counseling, 107,109
"Courage" (Bass), 97-98
Criticism, 119
 negative, 107,109
Cultural activities, 107,110

Death and dying
 anger related to, 13,71-73,74
 anxiety related to, 73-75
 euphemisms regarding, 27
 of family member, 15,69-79,137
 fear of, 13
Denial of Death (Becker), 22
Depression, 74
Dieting, 23-24
Dress code, 19,23

Eisley, Loren, 73
Ellis, Havelock, 43
Ellwood, Gracia Fay, 26
Envy, 119
Exercise, 107,108

Faith at Work, 111
Finances, 103-104
Finite-accepting behavior, 133

Forgiveness, 121-124
"For the Time Being" (Auden), 86
Friendship, 95,96-98,104,106,109
Funeral service, 65-66

Gehlen, Arnold, 43-44
*Getting Unstuck: Breaking Through
    the Barrier to Change*
    (Simon), 120
Goddess, 36
Grandmothers, 22
Gray Panthers, 100,105
*Great Cosmic Mother:
    Rediscovering the Religion of
    the Earth, The* (Sjöö and
    Mor), 133-134
Grief
  aging-related, 57-59
  bereavement-related, 77,78,79
Growing Young (Montagu), 41-44

Haldan, J.B.S., 43
Harris, William J., 51
Health, responsibility for, 104
Heroines, 99-101
Hoffman, Abbie, 9
Hofstetter, Adrian, 99,100
*Hungar Pains: The American
    Women's Tragic Quest for
    Thinness* (Pipher), 23-24

"If They Come in the Night"
    (Piercy), 48-49
In Memoriam (Tennyson), 86
Interdependence, 18
*I'm Running Away from Home But
    I'm Not Allowed to Cross the
    Street: A Primer of Women's
    Liberation* (Burton), 41

James, Alice, 86
James, Henry, 86
James, William, 119
Jewett, Sarah Orne, 82

Jung, Carl, 17

Kinsolving, Keith, 81
Kirkpatrick, Jean, 96
Kollman, Julius, 43
Kopp, Sheldon, 99,100
Kuhn, Maggie, 100-101

Labor force, women's participation,
    35
Lambert, Don, 52
Language, ageism and, 25-28
Larson, Bruce, 111
Layton, Elizabeth, 52
Legal matters, responsibility for,
    105
Leisure time, 104
Lewis, C.S., 123
Lieblein, Judy Claire, 97-98
Life-enhancing behavior, 133
Lifelines, 90
Lilly Endowment, Inc., 111
Living arrangements, 105
Loneliness, 50,105
Lorenz, Konrad, 43
Love, 17
Love relationship, 107,109
Lovett-Keen, Jan, 31

*Making Peace with Food: Freeing
    Yourself from the Diet/Weight
    Obsession* (Kano), 23
Mary Tyler Moore Show, 81
Media, portrayal of women by, 20
Mental health, risk-taking and, 111
Merton, Thomas, 79
Montagu, Ashley, 41-44
Moore, Jim, 125
Moore, Marianne, 124
Morley, Christopher, 127
Mother Teresa, 61,101

Neoteny, 41-42,45
Nelson, Gertrude, 92

Neibuhr, Reinhold, 97,123
Nutrition, 104-105,107,108

O'Keeffe, Georgia, 59
Older Women's League (OWL),25,
    105
Olson, Hertha, 90
Organizations, membership in, 105

Parents, forgiveness of, 121,122
Physical appearance, 3,5,19-24
    cultural factors affecting, 4,19-24,
        61,62,63
    as grief cause, 57-59
    sexuality and, 20,61
    youthful, 22-23,43
Pipher, Mary, 23-24
Politics of Women's Spirituality, The
    (Spretnak), 134
Porter, Mamie, 90
Positivism, 3-4,5,7-11,21
Power, 4-5,9,16,21,26-27,29,33,
    35-36,41,42,44,48,52,63,
    110,113,115,120,133

Regret, 7,9,85-87,89-92
Religion, 65-67
    patriarchal nature of, 65
Responsibility, 103-106
Risk-taking, 111-115
    emotional, 111,112-113
    intellectual, 111,113
    physical, 111,113
    spiritual, 111,113
Role models, 63,99-101
    friends as, 97
    self-esteem and, 119
Roles, of women, 3,33-37
Roosevelt, Eleanor, 101
Rubin, Jerry, 9

Salk, Jonas, 51
Sarton, May, 30,120
Schaef, Anne Wilson, 26-27

Seattle Older Woman's League, 15
Secular Organizations for Sobriety,
    96
Self-blame, 121-122
Self-development, 41-45
Self-doubt, 29
Self-esteem, 99,117,118,119
Self-knowledge, 47-52
Sexism, in advertising, 20
Sexuality, of older women, 20,61-62
Simon, Sidney, 111,117-118,
    119-120,121,122-123
Simon, Suzanne, 111,117-118,119,
    121,122-123
Sleep, 107
Solitude, 105,106,107,108
Starhawk, 55
Stoddard, Sally, 26
*Support Groups: It Doesn't Have to
    Be You Alone Against the
    World* (Twarogowski), 97
Support groups/systems, 95-98,134
    risk-taking and, 114

Terminal illness, of family member,
    69-76
Three Questions technique, 90
Time, as enemy, 126
Time, passage of, 81-83
Time management, 107,109
To Dance With God (Nelson), 92
Touching, 107,109
Transportation, 104
Travel, 104
Twarogowski, Janet, 97

United Nations Conference on
    Women, Forum 1985,
    134-135

Values clarification and realization
    theory, 79,117-120
Values and Teaching (Raths, Harmin
    and Simon), 119-120

Walpole, Hugh, 86
"Warning" (Joseph), 128
Weight, 20,23,24,57,62-63
Wellness, overall, 107-110
Wells, Ann, 132-133
Wilson, Elizabeth K., 90-91
Women for Sobriety, 96

Women's Campaign Fund, 9
Work, 33-37
    financial recompense for, 29

Youthfulness
    as cult, 21,42-43
    as human trait, 41-45

Life enhancing behavior

Models - ?